"This is not a book for the faint-hearted, but it is a book for anyone who wants to explore the depths of Christian commitment. Michael Phillips offers a much-needed corrective to several popular but superficial descriptions of the Christian life. He dares us to abandon all candy-coated versions of the gospel in order to experience the real gospel. His challenge is to go beyond admiring Jesus, even beyond praising Jesus, in order to resemble Jesus."

—BISHOP WILLIAM C. FREY, author of

The Dance of Hope

MAKE ME
LIKE JESUS

MICHAEL PHILLIPS

MAKE ME LIKE JESUS

THE COURAGE
TO PRAY DANGEROUSLY

WATERBROOK
PRESS

MAKE ME LIKE JESUS
PUBLISHED BY WATERBROOK PRESS
2375 Telstar Drive, Suite 160
Colorado Springs, Colorado 80920
A division of Random House, Inc.

ISBN 1-57856-674-6

Library of Congress Cataloging-in-Publication Data
Phillips, Michael R., 1946–
    Make me like Jesus : the courage to pray dangerously / Michael Phillips.—1st ed.
      p.   cm.
    ISBN 1-57856-674-6
    1. Christian Life. I. Title.
BV4501.3 .P48 2003
248.4—dc21   2002010802

Printed in the United States of America
2003—First Edition

10 9 8 7 6 5 4 3 2 1

CONTENTS

Other Books by Michael Phillips

God, A Good Father
Jesus, An Obedient Son
Destiny Junction
King's Crossroads
Hidden in Time
The Eleventh Hour

INTRODUCTION

This is not a book for everyone.

Time is a commodity we all prize. Therefore, to prevent you from exerting valuable energy on a message that does not interest you or that you are not ready for at this particular juncture in your life, I am going to offer several reasons why you should not read this book...and one very good reason why you should.

To decide not to proceed can sometimes be prudent. The single book that has had the greatest impact on my life more than any other originally came to me before I was ready for it. One day my spiritual mentor eagerly handed me the small volume and said it would change my life. In trying to read it, however, I found myself hopelessly bogged down within a few pages.

Disappointed, I took the book back to him. "I just couldn't get into it," I said. "I didn't even understand what the author was talking about."

"That's okay," my friend said. "Don't worry. Keep it a while longer. Put it aside. Another day will come, and then it will be right."

I did as he said...and indeed that *right* time arrived a couple years later.

Suddenly the book I had found boring and dry exploded with meaning. I couldn't put it down. I read it three or four times in continuous succession. Never before, and never since, have I encountered a book that so resonated with my spirit.

It was all in the rightness of the timing. I am so glad I waited.

Spiritual development cannot be rushed. There is no such thing as hothouse maturity. Wisdom takes time to be nurtured. God is never in a hurry. Recognizing this process at work, especially within oneself, prevents much frustration and impatience.

Therefore, if the circumstances do not seem right for you now to respond in a complete way to the principles with which this book is concerned, waiting until later may be the wisest course of action.

FOUR REASONS NOT TO READ THIS BOOK

Primarily I am writing to practicing Christians. If you have not yet reached that point in life where you are attempting daily to live according to the principles of the gospel of Jesus Christ as set forth in the Bible, then what follows will have little meaning for you. I recommend that you wait until such time as you *are* ordering your life according to his teachings and commands—for I believe such a time *will* come to you. Then perhaps you will remember this little book and will again seek out its life-changing truths for what they can offer you.

Not only do I write to Christians. This is a book for those who have been energetically devoted to their walk of faith for some time and who have made substantial progress toward maturity in that walk. There are many points of emphasis needed for new and relatively young Christian believers, and these are valuable assets in the early stages of growth. I have written on such important topics myself. But this is not such a book. If you are just starting out as a Christian, then what follows will not have the meaning for you that it will later. I recommend that you wait until such time that you find yourself hungering for greater depth in your walk with God. Perhaps then you will want to turn to this little book and will find it has greater meaning for you.

Spiritual development cannot be rushed.
God is never in a hurry.

As a brief footnote to the previous two points, and because of them, I will add that this book will not concern itself with the salvation experience nor make an attempt to discuss the Atonement. I assume that most will be past those stages in their own spiritual pilgrimages. I am continually surprised at the persistent criticism that comes from those who think that some form of the Four Spiritual Laws must turn up in every book a Christian writes. I have now penned a good many books, and I usually write to those who are already walking in faith. Invariably there are those who think I am not truly a Christian if I do not try to make sure my readers are saved every few chapters. I will not be doing so here. If you are uncomfortable with that, then this book is probably not for you.

Additionally, this is not a book about the corporate religious experience. We will not be exploring church fellowship, worship, relationships with others, and other issues of what is sometimes called "body life." I have written elsewhere on these topics. Instead, our focus here is on the *personal* imperative of faith, upon which the corporate experience must be based for it to have full eternal validity. I realize that there are many for whom, at present, the corporate outworking of religious activity is the primary emphasis. If you are among these, it is unlikely that what follows will contain the meaning it may at some later point in your individual pilgrimage, when the corporate experience is unable to satisfy deeper longings you find rising up in your heart.

Finally, this is a book for those whose spiritual hunger exceeds the blessings they hope to receive from their prayers, experiences, study, learning, and other spiritual pursuits. There are, of course, blessings that come to those who order their steps according to

God's principles. But walking in the footsteps of Jesus, and seeking the imprint of his knees in the soil of that ancient garden called Gethsemane, is not always the pathway to "blessing" according to the world's standard of measurement. Sadly, many Christians in the Western church do measure by that standard. They have forgotten the Lord's words. In our present culture of affluence and abundance, we no longer regard lashes from the whip or drops spilled by the crown of thorns as badges of honor in discipleship.

Therefore, if you are one who feels that the prayer for blessings is to be the focus of your energies, then no doubt this book will hold little interest for you. If so, I pray that a time will come in your life when the desire of your heart becomes not what God will do for *you*, or what blessings will come to *you*, or how *your* borders might be enlarged, but rather what *he* wants for you. Perhaps then you will remember this little book and will seek out its life-changing truths for what they can offer you.

ONE REASON TO CONTINUE

After these four preliminary cautions, there may be very few of you left reading my words. Books that promise the Christian blessings, like television programs of the same ilk, will always attract great throngs flocking to rejoice in the ease of their promised rewards. The crowds prefer joyful, hands-in-the-air "experience" to bending the knees in self-abandonment. Thus, the path toward Gethsemane will never be heavily trod. The prayer of Christlikeness, even among those calling themselves his followers, has never been a prayer for the multitudes. No shallow promises are given to those who venture there.

If you are one of those seeking the seclusion of that garden where obedience is perfected because you want to know God more intimately and live in his presence, let us embark together on an inward journey of the soul. Even if many others set this book aside after reading the above, it is my prayer that you are one who is tired of the Christianity of these modern times and finds yourself hungering for more. Therefore, even if this proves a solitary quest, it will be one richly rewarded—not with blessings capable of being seen with earthly eyes, but with the blessings of eternity.

Therefore, let us together seek God's purpose as, in the quietness of our hearts, we learn to whisper the sacred and holy prayers modeled for us by our Lord—through whom was perfected the salvation of the world.

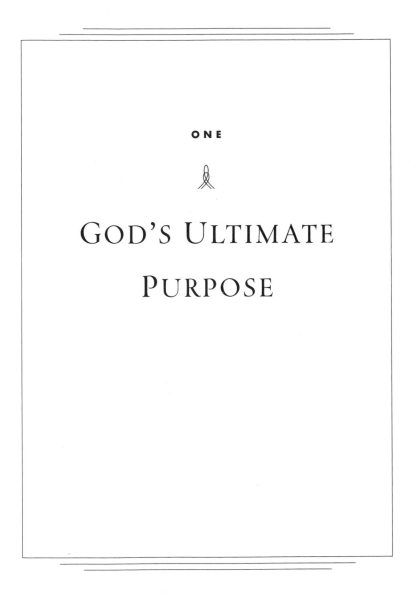

ONE

GOD'S ULTIMATE

PURPOSE

Some thirty-five years ago I began asking God to do something in my life. The consequences of that prayer I never could have foreseen. The request was an intensely personal one. It was not something to be taken lightly or talked about casually, even among one's closest spiritual companions. For years the only person I discussed it with was my wife, Judy. Later, when I had occasion to share it with a few others, I found to my amazement that some took offense at my presumption to even think along the lines they assumed were implied.

Some matters in the spiritual realm are best kept between oneself and the Lord. So from that point on I kept my mouth shut. I continued to talk to him about my request, discussing the slow progress of this particular one of his children. But to this day, he and Judy remain my sole confidants.

One thing I certainly never intended to do was write about it.

A BOOK I WOULD NEVER WRITE

In one sense I have never written a book in which this prayer did not play a foundational role in my thoughts. Never do I develop a character in one of my novels without this prayer operating as an unseen force between the lines. For me, *everything* in life revolves around this prayer—every relationship, how Judy and I raised our family, the books I write, how we relate to God, and especially how we view our own growth.

Not that I am thinking about it all the time. I am not consciously praying the words every minute any more than I consciously remind my lungs to breathe or my heart to beat. Yet, though my specific awareness of this prayer floats continually between my conscious and my subconscious mind, nothing is more foundational to my outlook, my belief system, and my walk with God. It forms the operational and daily bedrock of my faith…my very existence. After more than a third of a century, this prayer *is* who I am as a man. But I never planned to write about it directly or specifically.

There have been two reasons for this. First, I considered it too personal, too private, and perhaps too difficult to communicate through the medium of words, even for an author. I did not consider myself capable of conveying a thousandth of the essential imperative of this prayer. I considered its depths too complex to be translatable into words. I *felt* them…but I did not think it possible that I would be able to *say* them. Perhaps this was an aspect of faith that each man or woman had to discover for themselves.

Second, the dichotomy between the ideal represented by this

prayer and the daily reality of my own weak manhood is too glaringly apparent. The immaturity of my flesh, my worldly ambitions, my motives of self, my un-Christlike reactions, my anxieties, my impatience, my lack of trust...these all stand out like a sore thumb. One of the frustrating peculiarities of the Christian life is that the longer one is at it, the less progress one sees. The more one resists the flesh, the more devious that "old man" seems to become. It is usually the spiritual toddler who testifies to great strides of faith and maturity almost daily or weekly. The seasoned veteran in the wars of faith, however, has grown wise enough to recognize his own flesh for the subtle enemy it is and often despairs of seeing godliness reflected out of his heart.

The point is, I am so very, very aware these days of my failures, my weaknesses, my frailties, and my defects of character. I realize, of course, that no man or woman attains in this life to a level of spirituality that makes him or her worthy to speak about the high things of God. We are all sinners and hypocrites together in that sense, looking toward a higher reality than we are capable of living out in practice. That's part of the growth process. That's why a pastor or teacher or author is nothing more than one thirsty sinner telling another where to find water.

I recognized that principle at work. Yet still I shrunk from speaking more directly on this deeply personal subject. Such a message, I thought, ought to come from a bearded saint of old like George MacDonald or D. L. Moody or Charles Spurgeon. The outer look of my life has no aura of sainthood to validate the message, as has gathered like a spiritual mist around the memory of such men at the very mention of their names. I'm sure those who know me best recognize this all too well. Most of the people I encounter have no idea that such thoughts and prayers pulsate beneath the surface within me as I am going about the relationships and activities that comprise my days.

I am, in short, a very common and ordinary man. And I have long felt that the delivery of this message required someone of more extraordinary gifts than I possess, and even perhaps a more uncommon level of Christlikeness than is yet evident in my life.

It will be obvious that I changed my mind. To briefly explain that change in my outlook will hopefully get us started in a right direction so that our time together can be wisely used by God's Spirit to accomplish his purposes within each one of us.

First Things and Second Things

During the years of my walk with the Lord, I have watched as the evangelical church has become more and more preoccupied with the externals and blessings of the Christian walk of faith. This has grown in recent years to what seems almost an obsession to pray for increased blessings from God's hand, and it is of great concern to me. I fear many Christians are being encouraged to pray in the power of the *flesh* for temporal blessing rather than in the *spirit* of Christ for godliness of character.

Many will no doubt be shocked by that statement. Therefore, let me state with unequivocal clarity a truth that is rarely taught in our churches: It is possible to pray for things of *secondary* significance, and then, observing apparent answers to those prayers, wrongly assume them to be of *primary* importance within the framework of God's will.

Let me restate this principle from a different angle so there will be no mistaking it: *Blessings from the hand of God, even answers to prayer, do not necessarily confirm and validate those things prayed for as elements of primary importance in the economy of God.*

If we are praying for secondary things and are generally faithful in those prayers, God may indeed give us those secondary things…yet our enthusiasm over those answers may prevent us from looking to the *primary* things toward which he would rather we focus our prayers and our overall lives. If we are content to expend energy on secondary things and their attendant blessings, we may never penetrate the bull's-eye of God's will. A loving parent may give a child the birthday present he or she asks for—making a wish come true—while knowing that there are far greater gifts to be given: love, discipline, safety, trust, and wisdom. In the same way, though our prayers may hit what we aim at, and answers to those prayers may indeed result, those prayer-targets may be out on the fringes of God's central purposes.

Relishing in the blessings apparent in their lives, many miss the best God wants for his people.

Blessings in themselves do not necessarily indicate God's stamp of approval. Sometimes they are the result of hard work or the application of a biblical principle. You don't have to be in Germany long before you realize it is a nation that has been "blessed" financially. Is this God's doing or, in part, due to a law requiring a national tithe to the church along with an energetic and hard-working populace? Following God's principles will result in blessing—sometimes without God's active and specific involvement.

Sadly, a number of Christians misunderstand this principle. Wrongly taught by many in public ministry, these Christians may spend their spiritual lives on the periphery of God's purpose and never realize it. Some of the most vibrant Christian men and women and lively, growing churches are relishing in the blessings apparent in their lives…all the while missing the *best* God wants for his people.

My concern over this epidemic of *Bless-my-life-Lord* spirituality has prompted the book you are holding in your hand.

FASHIONING SONS AND DAUGHTERS

There are many secondary aspects of God's will that are good, right, and scriptural elements of spirituality with which we should be concerned. We do well to understand those and pray for God to develop them within us. Books and sermons and Bible studies and conferences by the thousands focus on this multitude of secondary things every day as we devote a lifetime of energy to various lesser elements of spirituality.

But what is God's *primary* will for his people?

Perhaps God wants to bless us. But is that his highest desire? What is it that God wants to do in your life, and in mine, above *all* other things?

What is the *summum bonum*—the greatest thing, the "supreme good" of life, the most perfect, ultimate purpose that is in God's mind and heart when he thinks of you and me?

It can be simply stated: That we become sons and daughters of God who are conformed to the image of Christ.

Jesus was *the* Son of God, the "only begotten" Son. God's design is that we, too, become sons and daughters, Christ's younger brothers and sisters, who are *like* him—who love like him, think like him, respond like him, resist the enemy like him, trust the Father like him, and who pray like him.

Without allowing ourselves to be sidetracked by the difficult doctrine of predestination, we find Paul probing straight to the heart of this divine intent in Romans 8:29: "For those whom he foreknew he also predestined to be conformed to the image of his Son, in order that he might be the first-born among many brethren" (RSV).

We will never be like him in his perfection, but God's purpose for you and me is that we become like Jesus in attitude, thought, and motive. Only *one* Son brought salvation to the world, but *all* of God's sons and daughters are to partake of that salvation by growing into the Christlikeness that it makes possible.

Obviously, this is a process—a *long* process, a lifelong process, because we *don't* naturally love or think or respond or trust God as Jesus did.

But make no mistake, the whole point of Christianity is to turn us into the kind of people who *can* do so—with tiny baby steps to begin with, then more steady steps as our lives progress. There is simply nothing else that the Christian life is about. Though we will never become perfectly like Jesus in this life, it is toward this end that God is leading us, and toward this divine "center" that the prayer of Christlikeness aims us.

It will be obvious that such a transformation into men and women who reflect the nature of Jesus Christ is not something that can be accomplished externally. Christians these days are fond of external proclamations. But we're talking here about something entirely different from what can be achieved through a bumper sticker or a worship service or a thirty-day program.

God's purpose for you and me is that we become like Jesus in attitude, thought, and motive

---

The kind of sonship and daughterhood that is in God's heart to accomplish will not come about by outward manifestation. It can happen only inwardly, as we become people of a certain nature and character.

God wants more than mere believers. He wants more than mere worshipers. He wants more than people who can parrot back doctrinally correct spiritual phrases. He wants more than men and women forever seeking new experiences and highs and blessings.

He is in the enterprise of fashioning sons and daughters.

In the same way that he stooped down and created Adam and

Eve from the dust of the ground, he similarly takes each of us when we give our lives to him and, to the extent that we yield to his remaking process, begins to fashion children who will one day bear the image and reflect the nature of his firstborn Son, Jesus Christ.

TWO

THE PRAYER OF CHRISTLIKENESS

"Make me like Jesus."

We now return to the request I made years ago, when I began asking God to conform me to the image of his Son.

I prayed: *God, make me like Jesus.*

I call this the prayer of Christlikeness. It is not a prayer to be prayed frivolously. If such a prayer has not been an active part of your prayer life prior to this point, I would encourage you not to pray it yet, not until you read on.

THE BULL'S-EYE OF FAITH

If a single element exists in the Christian life where counting the cost is imperative, it is in the praying of this prayer.

Be very clear, there *is* a cost involved in becoming more like Jesus Christ. A heavy cost.

If you don't mean business with God, you will only slow your spiritual progress by praying the prayer of Christlikeness. The words seem simple enough. But the means by which it is answered are anything but simple.

The prayer of Christlikeness truly represents the ultimate

road less traveled. It is a pilgrimage that, if undertaken seriously and reaffirmed daily, will change everything. It will set you on a course apart from the crowd, even the "spiritual" crowd. In quiet and subtle ways you will find yourself diverging even from many in your own church. As your outlook and the priorities of your heart begin to shift, you will recognize that you are on a journey different from that of most within the religious multitude.

> *The prayer of Christlikeness truly represents the ultimate road less traveled.*

Teachings that sugarcoat the gospel message by telling self-absorbed Christians what they want to hear, and ignore all those unpleasant things like self-denial and putting others first, will always find a receptive public. Of course people love such messages. Who wouldn't rather be told that God wants us eating chocolate-chip cookies and cherry pie rather than broccoli and Brussels sprouts? Scarce wonder that the most popular teachings today are those that promise the greatest blessings and make us feel good about ourselves.

It's all the fun and joy and blessing of Christianity, without the cost. It all goes down so easily. Being told that God wants for us exactly what our flesh wants too is the magic pill upon which dozens of ministries are based. It's a little like a spiritual lottery ticket, a variation of the old God-wants-you-rich doctrine with which the Enemy has had so much success in the contemporary evangelical church.

But it's not a teaching that proceeds from the mouth of Jesus.

WHAT KIND OF STRENGTH DOES IT TAKE?

When I began praying the prayer of Christlikeness, I knew that it was a lifetime enterprise. But I did not really count the cost either. I had no way of doing so.

Where it would lead, I had no idea. There have been occasional moments since when I have faced such depths of discouragement and despair that I have come within a hair's breadth of taking it back, of shouting, "God, forget it. I will always believe, but I no longer want to be like Jesus. I no longer want to follow him to the cross. Remove your hand from me!"

At such times I have been conscious of standing before a cliff, almost ready to jump off, reminded of our Lord's third temptation. But each time I have stepped back and, in tears of anguish, reaffirmed the prayer—though there have been times when it has been so difficult that my stomach physically ached as I did so.

The prayer of Christlikeness is no prayer for the spiritually fainthearted. When I say that, I do not mean it is only for the strong and self-assured. I am not strong. I am no great man of faith. Perhaps I am a little stubborn. It has been my determination to see the prayer through to the end that has driven me time and again to my knees in tears, once more to reaffirm, in my *weakness* not my strength: "Father…whatever it takes…I am willing…create in me the heart of a true son…and make me like Jesus."

Even as I completed that sentence and my fingers stilled, the words I had written assaulted me again with their difficulty…nay, their impossibility. I found myself staring out my window, facing again, as so many times before, the heavy *cost* of that prayer.

Whatever it takes, I am willing…
Create in me the heart of a true son…
Make me like Jesus.

I just sat staring. I had written the words *for you*…but could I pray the prayer again *for me?* Not in the abstract, but today, right now, this very moment?

The cost…the *cost*…lay heavy upon my heart.

Finally I got out of my chair and slowly sank to my knees. At first the only sound that came was a deep sigh that I'm sure, after all these years, the Lord knows how to translate into his heart.

Then I tried to pray the prayer I had just written—not so that I could tell you about it (I was not even thinking that far ahead at the time), but because I knew I *had* to pray it yet again. I could not tell anyone else to pray it if I could not pray it.

Another moment had come in which the Lord was saying to me, as he does periodically, *"Are you still willing to follow me all the way?"*

Then I tried to pray. But as I did, I could not even say the words, "I am willing." What came out of my mouth was, "Whatever it takes…I think I am willing…I will try to be willing, Lord… I *want* to be willing…help me be willing…"

Then came another long pause. I thought the prayer would be easy. It used to be so much easier. But the cost is ever present before me. I know a little more what it means now…and the hill to which this prayer must always lead.

I sighed again, then finally whispered, "Father…make me like Jesus."

I try never to write in the abstract, whether it is a novel or a book such as this. If the challenges of faith I lay before my readers are not those with which I am continually probing the shadowy recesses of my own heart, then my words are meaningless. I write as a way of sharing my own inner journey. Some of my readers occasionally pick up on that. Hopefully I can encourage and bolster the steps of a few others along the way.

Such has been my own struggle these last five minutes. Therefore, it was hard to pray those words. I was not filled with joy when I rose back to my feet. What in my youthful exuberance was a prayer of hope and enthusiasm has become for me now a prayer of obedience.

I have been asking God to develop Christlikeness within me for thirty-five years. It is sometimes difficult to see much headway. But I continue to pray it. Sometimes it is very, very difficult to say the words. In the last four years it has become more difficult than ever because of a crisis that appears to have been caused, in part, by my attempt to make this prayer real in our family.

Yes, the cost is heavy. Judy and I struggle with that cost every day. At this point in our pilgrimage with God, it is not always, as I say, with joyful hearts that we pray this prayer.

It is a quiet prayer, a personal prayer, a humbling prayer, an invisible prayer.

It can be a lonely prayer, a painful prayer, a sacrificial prayer. One cannot pray this prayer anywhere but at the altar.

Yet nothing else so represents the bull's-eye of faith. Not that one ever hopes to actually arrive at such a mountain peak of complete oneness with God. Our failure is implied by the very prayer itself. We pray it *because* we will never attain to it. The very uttering of the words contains the admission that we will never reach anything close to Christlikeness in this life. But if you don't aim at the center of the target, how will you get close?

Is it, therefore, presumptuous to say such words?

Not if we pray it in weakness and in full recognition of our weakness.

Paul wrote to the Philippians, "Not that I have already obtained all this, or have already been made perfect, but I press on to take hold of that for which Christ Jesus took hold of me.... I press on toward the goal" (3:12,14).

That is what the prayer represents—pressing on toward the *center* of God's purpose.

Likeness to Christ.

THE SCISSORS OF SANCTIFICATION

The prayer of Christlikeness is not a prayer that can be answered by fiat, with a magic wand.

How does God answer it?

He answers through *our* willingness—our willingness to become sons and daughters of self-denying obedience. God cannot effect the transformation without the bowed head, bent knees, and empty hands of our own obedience.

When we pray, "Father, make me like Jesus," we must be clear that it is not a prayer God can answer without our taking an equal share in the process.

We are not *made* like Jesus, we must *become* like Jesus.

How does the change take place? Who is responsible for it?

It comes as we yield our human nature to the Father, exactly as Jesus did. It comes as, one by one, little bits of the *self-nature* are snipped off so that the *Christ-nature* can emerge in their place. The more of self that is cut away and removed as a source of motive, attitude, thought, and action, the more room grows within us for the Spirit of Christ to determine motive, attitude, thought, and action.

Again we ask, "But *how* is self-centeredness thus snipped from that innermost part of us where the source of rule is determined?"

God has provided a divine instrument to carry out this job of cutting away self so that Christ can shine out. It is not, however, a *one-man* instrument of sanctification, as many suppose, which God wields by himself to carry out the operation. It is no single-handled scalpel that he alone uses to conduct the needful surgery. We can pray the prayer of Christlikeness all our lives and nothing will happen if we simply lay on the operating table and expect God to do all the cutting. Indeed, this is a very different kind of surgery. In this operation, the patient has to help the Physician because the surgical instrument requires two people. It is a double-handled pair of spiritual scissors.

They are the scissors of *command* and *obedience*.

How these scissors function—gradually putting self to death, steadily cutting its influence out of motive, attitude, thought, and action—is one of the least-apprehended aspects of the walk of faith. We must wield one handle while God holds the other.

We are not made like Jesus, we must become like Jesus.

This is growth indeed—a growth toward *less* rather than toward *more!*

To cut away motives of self, to cut away unkindness, to cut away wrong attitude, to cut away unforgiveness…we must work together with God. He cannot remove them by himself. He has determined that Christlikeness requires an active, not passive, commitment on our part.

To ask which of the two blades is most important, or which actually carries out the "cutting" self-crucifying work, is as pointless as asking which blade of an ordinary pair of scissors actually *cuts* the cloth. They work together or they don't work at all.

BLESSING OR CHRISTLIKENESS

Perhaps this obedience I speak of, these painfully snipping scissors of sanctification, do not sound to you like much fun. If your perspective is that "the kingdom of God is a party" as many believe today—a tragic development in the history of the church that has quite possibly set back the Lord's coming indefinitely—then you are reading the wrong book. You will not find that perspective in the Gospels or find me pampering your soulish nature with promises of the very things your flesh desires. Dying for one's faith, crucifying the flesh, and even the martyrdom of the centuries no longer seem to fit into the agenda of the modern evangelical church.

If spiritual maturity is one's goal, it seems to me that praying for blessings for oneself is something of a backward approach. Jesus did not pray that blessing would come to him. He prayed, rather, to do his Father's will. Jesus said we must *deny* the flesh, not indulge it with prayers that continue to feed it.

There are many aspects of the Old Testament that we can learn from, but that we must recognize as only partial truth as seen through a glass darkly. Praying that God would slaughter one's enemies and increase the size of one's flocks was, in many respects, a temporal prayer, gratifying to the flesh but not necessarily eternally sustaining to the spirit. The incomplete imagery of the Old Testament must not supplant the new wine the Son of God brought wherewith to fill us. Hebrews 1:1-2 is the lens through which we must interpret and clarify Old Testament truth: "In the past God spoke to our forefathers through the prophets at many times and in various ways, but in these last days he has spoken to us by his Son."

Readers often tell me that my books and the themes within them are for the few, not the many. Perhaps they are right. That such a distinction exists within Christendom has always baffled me, though I see its evidences throughout history and around me every day. Why do not *all* God's people want their growth to be characterized by obedience? What else is there to life but that? Why would anyone want other than to press all the way to the utmost pinnacle of relationship with God?

But I suppose none of us wants to walk the Calvary road as much as we think we do. I am surely no exception. It has always been easier to *talk* about dying to self than to actually die to self, to *talk* of obedience than to obey, to *talk* of crucifying the flesh than to crucify the flesh. So perhaps there will always be the few and the many, and even among the few there will be the few and the many, and none of us is as committed in our discipleship as we will someday wish we had been. How painful it will be to realize how short we came of living among the true "few," among the likes of Peter and Stephen and Paul and so many of that early generation, as well as those of successive generations who gave their all and took discipleship to the very limits of earthly obedience.

Three

THE PRAYER OF CHILDSHIP

"Father, what would you have me do?"

Dedicating oneself to the prayer of Christlikeness begins a lifetime of growth. At whatever point one first prays it and means it down to the deepest marrow of the will—whether that moment comes at age twenty or eighty—all priorities, motives, attitudes, ambitions, and perspectives change. Some of these changes are immediate and visible. Most are silent, invisible, and slow to develop.

Many Christians talk a great deal about "growth." It is one of the most commonly discussed aspects of the Christian life. But in connection with the prayer of Christlikeness, we are speaking of something vastly different from the accumulation of spiritual knowledge that usually goes by that name. We are seeking spiritual *reality*, not knowledge.

What those around you call growth usually indicates an increase of what they consider their storehouse of wisdom. The "old man" delights in filling those soul-granaries full to overflowing.

As for you, what you call growth will instead be toward *less* of anything to which your flesh can cling for survival. Whatever exalts your *self* you will now view as a step backward rather than forward.

The fact is, when we begin to pray, "Father, make me like Jesus," we are no longer our own. That cannot help but change everything, though the world—especially those closest to you—will likely see no change at all.

Every motive is now imbued with new significance, new perspective, new imperative. To respond as Jesus responded suddenly floods into being as the illuminating purpose that gives everything in life definition and meaning. It goes far beyond merely wearing a bracelet that reads, *What would Jesus do?* We are not seeking to *say* it…we are seeking to *do* it.

---

*The most important paths to spiritual maturity
are invisible to human eyes.*

Too often in the history of Christendom, the gulf between these two—our *say* and our *do*—has been the precipitous void in which the mighty truths of God have ignominiously fallen, there to be lost altogether to the world's vision.

But it shall not be so among those who dedicate themselves to the prayer of Christlikeness. They themselves know how short they fall. Thus they make no ostentatious proclamations of Christlikeness. They reserve their talk about doing what Jesus would do for their own private closets of prayer.

They are not seeking for their Christlikeness to be seen. They are all too aware of the delusion of visible piety.

They know that the most important paths to spiritual maturity are invisible to human eyes.

PERFECT SON OF A PERFECT FATHER

From the prayer of Christlikeness, therefore, the very practical question immediately arises: How is it to be done, this high and holy thing? How do we—how *can* we—possibly appropriate the Christlike life for ourselves?

Can one hope to attain to any practical level of actually doing, living, responding, behaving, and thinking...*like Jesus?*

Astonishingly, the answer is a resounding *yes!*

We can be like him in that most important of ways in which his own Sonship was lived out. We can turn our hearts to the Father, as Jesus did.

With Jesus we can say, *Father, what would you have me do?*

And with that chosen subservience, the prayer of childship, we indeed make ourselves one with Christ.

Now it is obvious that Jesus did not need to pray for Christlikeness. He *was* Christ—the perfect Son of God. It was not

necessary for him to pray for it—the truth of it was already alive
in him. But what was it that made him Christlike? Of what was
his Christlikeness comprised? What made him a Son?

The answer lies in the question itself. He was the perfect *Son*
of the perfect *Father.*

This means neither more nor less than this: Jesus was an obedient *child.* He did what his Father wanted him to do, not what
he wanted to do himself. He took his Father's will into himself
and replaced his own will with that greater Father-will.

In the example of that childness, we discover the doorway that
leads toward Christlikeness for ourselves.

Listen carefully to the words of childness from Jesus' own
mouth as recorded in the gosepl of John:

I seek not to please myself, but him who sent me.

I do the work of the Father.

The Son can do nothing by himself; he can do only what
he sees his Father doing, because whatever the Father does
the Son also does.

I have come in my Father's name.

I live because of the Father.

I am not alone. I stand with the Father, who sent me.

I do nothing on my own, but speak just what the Father has taught me...I always do what pleases him.

I honor my Father.

I and the Father are one.

Whatever I say is just what the Father has told me to say.

It is the Father, living in me, who is doing his work.

The Father is greater than I.

The world must learn that I love the Father and that I do exactly what my Father has commanded me.

I have obeyed my Father's commands and abide in his love.

I am not alone, for my Father is with me.

Do these sound like the declarations of an independently minded man who determined his own way in life?

Of course not. They are the words of a child. A man...but a man who had decided to subserve that manhood to the greater privilege of conducting his affairs in childship.

A CHOSEN CHILDSHIP

The truly startling thing about these statements of submission become apparent when we recognize that Jesus was not forced into his role in the divine drama that resulted in the world's salvation.

He *chose* his Sonship.

He had to *choose* to submit his way to the Father's will, just as we do. He confronted this decision not just once or twice, but ten thousand times, over and over, all day, every day...all his earthly life. It didn't "just happen."

Pause a moment to allow the wonder of it to sink in.

God, give us hearts capable of receiving this incredible reality for the practical, life-empowering truth it can be...for each one of us!

What else is the prayer of childness—though modernism hates the word—but a prayer of submission?

Jesus was not a Son because he could not help it. In the midst of a fully human mortality, he *chose* to be a child. His every breath, every thought, every action, was both a prayer and a living out of that prayer: *Father, what would you have me do?*

There are those who would make of Jesus an angel—a being without free will. If most men and women were to analyze it, I think they would find in their minds a sort of half-man, half-angel occupying the central role in the gospel story.

But Jesus was born a complete man. No angel wings. No halo around his head. His was a physical and mortal body. His was a human will. He got tired. He sweat. He went to the bathroom. He had to wash his hair and his hands and his feet. His brain possessed the capacity to think. He had emotions that loved, got irritated at his disciples and angry at the Pharisees, and became fearful for what he had to face as the Cross neared.

Most important, he was born with a fully developed *free will* of humanity.

This was no glow-in-the-dark Son of God whose Sonship came any other way than ours must come. He was a Son because he *chose* to be a Son.

Now in truth he was God-man, the Divine Man. But we mustn't let his divinity obscure the totality of his manhood. We can't imagine that he brought along a tiny magic wand into the manger at Bethlehem to pull out when the going got rough or to make sure no sin could get too close to him or temptation bite too dangerously deep. It wasn't a cute little baby angel that Mary held in her arms, a being *incapable* of sin because of his heavenly origins. The enormity of Christ's Saviorhood is found in this—that it is born out of a manhood that *chose* to be our Redeemer. Mary held a tiny *boy* in the swaddling clothes of the incarnation...*her* own son and *God's* own Son.

Then Jesus grew in wisdom and in stature and in favor with God and man. And as he grew he continually humbled himself, emptied himself, living out the full expression of his being as a man with free will.

"For the divine nature was his from the first; yet he...emptied himself, taking the very nature of a slave. Bearing the human likeness, revealed in human shape, he humbled himself and became obedient..." (Philippians 2:6-7, NEB, NASB, NIV).

Amid the urge to exalt self, only a mortal can *choose* childship.

No angel can make such a choice. That's why God did not merely send an angel to announce the kingdom of God. He sent his Son to show us how to live in that kingdom.

We had to do more than just hear the message. We had to *see* it. We had to know that it could be done, that the mortal will of *self* really could submit itself to One higher.

An angel might have been able to *tell* us. Only a man could *show* us.

So God became a man.

Not a pretend man or a partial man…but a *real* man. With real struggles. With a real will that wanted its own way.

It becomes all too easy to gloss over the humanity of Jesus, thinking it was somehow easier for him to lay down his will. But as Jesus grew and matured, his will developed fully as a *human* will. He *wanted* his own way, just as you and I do. And no sin exists in wanting one's way—for that cannot be helped—but only in choosing our way over God's way. Laying down his will was anything but automatic for Jesus. His was no cheap death to self, no easy relinquishment, no automatic abandonment of self-rule. It involved no mere figurative "blood, sweat, and tears," but the *real* blood, the *real* sweat, and the *real* tears of genuine manhood.

He did not enter into the fullness of Sonship all at once in Bethlehem. He had to *become* a Son by the exercise of his free will, capable in the end of laying down his life for the sins of the world.

THE HIGHEST IS ALWAYS TO GIVE

What makes the life given to mankind so unique? The gift of a free and independent *will*. This will is the deepest, strongest thing in man, our link with God himself.

Think what God did. He created beings that were *like* him,

yet *separate* from him. So separate, in fact, as to be capable of choosing or *not* choosing to walk in fellowship with him.

Free will is simply the most remarkable aspect of all creation! It is the only thing truly ours, completely our very own. For, having given it to us, God, in a sense, bound the hands of his own omnipotence to interfere with it. What each of us will do with this priceless possession is the great drama of eternity.

Naturally, then, comes the question: What is the highest thing one can do with God's gift of free will?

I would contend that it is this: to give it away.

Because the highest is always to *give*. It is why the most far-reaching love involves sacrifice. To give most deeply always means one must give oneself. "For God so loved the world that he *gave*" (John 3:16).

What is the highest thing one can do with God's gift of free will?

To give, to yield, to give away, even to give up…such comprise the ingredients of the highest forms of love we know.

We return, then, to the will. Not just any "will," an abstract will…but *your will and my will*. What is the highest, the deepest, the ultimate thing we can each do with our will?

Yield it...abandon it...sacrifice it...and *give it back* to our Creator and Father who gave it to us in the first place.

We know this is the highest because it is exactly such a yielding of the human will that we witness in the life of Jesus.

FREEDOM OF CHOICE CAN GO EITHER WAY

The implication of chosen childship—*Father, what would you have me do?*—is perhaps greater than most of us realize.

If there is true choice, complete *free* will...then the outcome of any decision can go either way. There are always two answers—yes or no.

Think what this means. When Jesus came to earth, his decisions, too, could have gone either way!

Salvation wasn't assured until Jesus breathed his last and gave up his mortality. For thirty-three years, in a sense, the fate of the world's salvation might be said to have hung in the balance.

Am I saying that Jesus *could* have failed?

Does the question almost ring with blasphemy?

I am not afraid to ask such questions because they probe deep into the reality of the prayer of childship. If we are not willing to make that prayer real, painfully real, stripping it of pious gloss, then we might as well not pray it. Spiritual life is either reality or a sham.

Father, what would you have me do? has no meaning unless we have a will of our own that can be in opposition to that Father-will—indeed, usually *is* in opposition to it.

The prayer of childship has no meaning unless there is indeed a *self-will* and a *Father-will*…and unless the freedom exists to choose either.

Jesus was a man with a fully functioning human will. By definition this means that, to the very cross, his own personal human will remained alive. At any point he could have said to his Father, "I want your will no longer…forget it…I'm on my own now!"

Therefore, I believe that Jesus could have failed. He did not *have* to choose the Father-will. That he did so, and did so perfectly, makes the Saviorhood of his divine Sonship all the more precious.

Jesus' Sonship was won through chosen obedience…chosen submission. So must ours be.

DEATH TO SELF AS MOTIVE

To pray the prayer of childship is impossible without our will willing God's will—without our exerting our own decision-making and attitude-forming will to consciously *choose* God's will in place of our own. To pray it and truly mean it involves nothing short of death to self as motive—death to all that self would do or want or think.

"Father, what would you have me do?" implies, "I die to all that I *myself* would do. I willingly lay down all that represents *my* will, not just now, today, but forever. I take instead *your* will for mine." This is how the Christ-life becomes ours.

George MacDonald writes:

The life of Christ is this—that he does nothing, cares for nothing for his own sake, because he cares with his whole soul for the will, the pleasure of his Father. Because his Father is his Father, therefore he will be his child.

Loving his Father with his whole being...he has gained the power to awaken life, the divine shadow of his own, in the hearts of his brothers and sisters, who have come from the same birth-home as himself, namely, the heart of his God and our God, his Father and our Father....

Jesus rose at once to the height of his being, set himself down on the throne of his nature, in the act of subjecting himself to the will of the Father as his only good, the only reason for his existence...he completed and held fast the eternal circle of his existence in saying, "Thy will, not mine, be done!" He made himself what he is by deathing himself into the will of the eternal Father, through which he was the eternal Son—thus plunging into the fountain of his own life, the everlasting Fatherhood.

This life, self-willed in Jesus, is the one thing that makes such life—the eternal life, the true life, possible—nay, imperative, essential, to every man, woman, and child....

There is no life for any man, other than the same kind that Jesus has; his disciple must live by the same absolute devotion of his will to the Father's.[1]

THE STILL, SMALL VOICE

How all of this works out in practice is very practical and very difficult.

The opportunity comes to pray the prayer of childship every day, with every decision we confront, with every attitude that creeps into our brain. But I would not trivialize it by implying that we are to pray, "God, do you want me to go to school today?" "Do you want me to be faithful to my obligations?" "Do you want me to do my work?" "Should I be unselfish toward those I meet?" In the pages of his Word, he has already made his will clear regarding the way we are to conduct ourselves. We don't need to pray about whether we should keep our promises, do our work diligently, be unselfish, or forgive someone who has wronged us.

---

1. George MacDonald, "The Creation in Christ," *Unspoken Sermons, Third Series* (Eureka, Calif.: Sunrise Books, 1996), 10-2.

The prayer of childship comes when we genuinely do not know what we are to do, when we need specific guidance about which decision to make, which course of action to follow, which of several alternatives to take. When there is no clear scriptural direction before us, then "Father, what would you have me do?" is a very practical prayer indeed. Then arrives the moment to be quiet and listen for the still, small voice of the Father's answer.

Detecting that voice is not easy. It takes years of practice to distinguish it from many counterfeit voices by which the flesh speaks in pious and lofty tones and pretends to be speaking on the Spirit's behalf. The motives of the cunning self will don a thousand masquerades to convince us that the Spirit of God is speaking when the voice is actually that of the self-indulgent flesh.

Occasionally the two wills may point in the same direction. But probably not as often as we like to think.

The most pivotal moments of childship that in large measure characterize our walk with God come when the will of the Father and the will of the child are not pointed in the same direction but are pitted one against the other. Out of that struggle the deepest childship is born.

Be very wary, my friends, when the voice you seem to be hearing confirms what you yourself want. It *may* be the Lord's voice. But when the Spirit speaks in a way that must lead to a crucifying of the flesh, your flesh will resist it tooth and nail and will do all in its power to prevent your hearing that quiet word. Heed the words of Jesus to those who would be his disciples: "If anyone would come after me, he must deny himself and take up his cross and follow me" (Mark 8:34).

Years ago an opportunity came to us to purchase an established retail business. The instant I learned of it my adrenalin began to pump, for it represented a plum in the plans I cherished for expansion. This would be a major acquisition that would greatly extend the reach of our business and almost double our sales volume. I wanted that store so badly I could taste it.

The most pivotal moments of childship come when the will of the Father and the will of the child are pitted against the other.

So even as I began to pray, "Lord, what is your will? What would you have us do?" in the back of my mind I was drawing up an offer.

Do you see the subtlety with which my flesh crept in even in the midst of my prayer? I was praying, yes, but praying in the direction of what *I* wanted.

I was in exactly that dangerous position I spoke of before. To all appearances I was seeking God's guidance. But the momentum of my *own* motives and my *own* will was so strong that, had the Lord had something else in mind, I'm not sure his still, small voice would have been able to get through even with a bullhorn at my ear. Besides, bullhorns are not usually God's way. He rarely forces his will upon us by contesting with our own wills in a shouting match. He leaves us to choose.

What I was really seeking was not so much divine guidance as divine *confirmation* for something I wanted. When confirmation is what we're after, it's not difficult to spin circumstances and daily occurrences to make them indicate just about anything.

As I look back, I'm not sure who was speaking through the various "signs" that seemed to confirm that we should go ahead with the purchase—God or my own will.

So I moved forward, made an offer, and anticipated the acquisition with expectant vision, signing a large long-term note for half the purchase price.

I do not say that God *was* leading or was *not* leading. I'm not really sure. In many aspects of my life, the passage of years reveals my flesh more and more clearly. I look back on many circumstances of the past with eyes a little less prone to spiritualize what I see. But neither am I anxious to explain away occasions when God has genuinely moved and revealed his direction to me, for to do so would be an equally great error. I am trying to be honest with myself these days, and honest with the Lord, and therefore honest with you.

My only conclusion about this transaction is that I took for God's answer the same thing I wanted anyway. Any non-Christian or someone not praying at all might have come to exactly the same decision. There was nothing uniquely Christlike about what I did. There was nothing to distinguish my action from what people in the world do every day when they buy and sell businesses. I prayed, yes, but there was no *childship* evident in either my prayer or my decision to go ahead because I remained in *my* will. At no time did I step out of my own will in order to step into *God's* will.

Perhaps, as a result, things did not go quite as well as I had expected. Within a few years I began to recognize that the expansion of our business was not what the Lord wanted. This was a painful realization. I could not foresee what he had on the horizon with my writing. I simply knew that he was prompting me to scale back. The voice was now at my ear and I was hearing it, and I began to feel the tension between my own will and "Father, what would *you* have me do?" At last I was slowly learning about childship.

Therefore, several years after the purchase, we sold this store that had become the cornerstone of our whole business. At the time, a sizable percentage of the original price remained outstanding on the note to the original owners, which our buyer assumed in taking over. We also carried a large portion of the new purchase price.

Within two years under the new owners, the business failed. They did not follow through with their commitments, blamed us for their failure, and after draining the business of most of its resources, simply stopped paying us and closed the doors. We were left with a financial disaster on our hands.

Now I really began to pray! It was far too late to salvage the store. In desperation, my request for guidance now became, "Lord, help!"

My flesh dreamed up all kinds of scenarios, legalities, and lawsuits justifying refusal to pay debts that technically shouldn't have been ours. By now I was so despondent that God's still, small voice was getting through loud and clear. And I didn't like what I heard. The words were: *Honor your commitments. Don't fight. Give it up.*

I have never hated the answer to a prayer so much.

My flesh didn't want to walk away. I wanted to fight, to stand up for our rights, to make sure everyone knew we had been taken advantage of. And I certainly didn't want to have to resume payments on the note to the original owners because of the default of our buyers, especially now that there wasn't even a business left to be paying on!

To give in would sink the rest of our business and possibly send us into bankruptcy. It seemed that doing what I felt the Lord telling me to do would amount to signing the death warrant of everything we had built up for more than a decade.

But still came the answer: *Lay it down. Be faithful. Walk away…and trust me.*

My flesh really didn't like it! Now indeed did I feel the price of the prayer of Christlikeness. How willing was I to be a child? My flesh came kicking and screaming to the altar, dreaming up every excuse to leave some piece of my pride and some portion of our balance sheet intact…justifications…legal arguments… everything in the book titled *It Isn't Fair!*

"Father, what do you want me to do?" had become a prayer in which my flesh and the Father's will stood in glaring contrast. *My* will and *God's* will were now pointed in two opposite directions. The exciting triumph of buying the business several years before had turned into a Gethsemane moment. My prayer of childship often sounded like, "God, I don't want to do this thing! Please give me some other way out."

When the moment of relinquishment came, and I finally said, "Okay, Lord, I will lay my will on the altar and do as you say," it was no moment of victory. I cannot sugarcoat the experience—it was a painful moment of death. It hurt. So many dreams and goals and hopes died within me as I finally relinquished what I wanted into God's hands. I knew that even if our business survived, we would be years climbing out of the debt. But I just had to lay it down, say, "Here, Lord, this is all yours now," and continue to pay off the debts even though no more income would be coming in from that store.

Why were these such difficult things to lay on the altar? I don't know. Probably because of my pride. It was an agonizing prayer to pray. I wept over it. Yet from it I learned something about the prayer of childship that perhaps I could not have learned any other way. God knows. I don't expend great efforts trying to understand everything that happened. If God understands, that is good enough for me. It still hurts to recall the episode. Childship is not a peaches-and-cream life. Sometimes there is pain, and I have known plenty of it in trying to make the prayer of Christlikeness real in my heart.

From this experience it seems appropriate that we now move on to consider a critical moment that often comes in the life of the disciple who has committed to pray dangerously. I call such crossroads "Gethsemane moments."

FOUR

THE PRAYER OF RELINQUISHMENT

"Not my will, but yours be done."

Each successive stage in the prayer of Christlikeness contains steadily deepening consequences.

I first prayed the prayer of Christlikeness without fully counting the cost. But once that prayer led me to the prayer of childship and a way of life dictated by the prayer, *Father, what would you have me do?* nothing in life was mine to determine again.

In making myself a child, I had submitted myself to the will of Another. Even though, as I have indicated, it took me years to learn how to pray that prayer in the self-denying way in which Jesus prayed it, such has been the course upon which I set myself many years ago.

CONSEQUENCES OF CHRISTLIKENESS

So, then, the prayer of childship also has consequences. This progression is clearly visible in the gospel account.

The first command is always to follow.

"Follow me," says Jesus. "Watch me, listen to me, learn of me, so that you can act, think, respond, and behave as I do."

But then the progression of deepening consequences continues. The disciples must now discover who Jesus is. Who is this man they have followed?

The second phase of discipleship training, therefore, occupies the ageless question to which all roads lead in the end: *Who is Jesus Christ?*

Each disciple must confront that eternal query in the depths of his or her own soul—you and me along with Peter, John, Andrew, and Judas. *Who is Jesus Christ…in my life?*

And what should we discover but that he is a Son?

"Who do men say that I am?" Jesus asks.

"You are the Christ, the *Son…*" resounds the answer upon which all of history hinges.

The steps that would follow Christlikeness, therefore, always and inevitably lead to the prayer of childness…to sonship. And what does sonship mean? Jesus tells us.

He then began to teach them that the Son of Man must suffer many things and be rejected by the elders, chief priests and teachers of the law, and that he must be killed and after three days rise again.…

"If anyone would come after me, he must deny himself and take up his cross and follow me. For whoever wants to

save his life will lose it, but whoever loses his life for me
and for the gospel will save it." (Mark 8:31,34-35)

The progression of discipleship leads to nothing more and
nothing less than the cross.

"PETER...WE ARE GOING TO DIE"

How much are we willing to lay down? How far are we willing to
follow?

What are the limits of the lordship we turn over to Christ?
What will we hold back? What pet lizards will we keep alive? How
much of our *selves* will we try to preserve intact?

The implication presented by the prayer of relinquishment is
stark and unyielding: Are you willing to give everything into the
Father's hands...even unto death?

Therefore, the decisive question always arrives: *What are you
ultimately going to do with the freedom of choice I gave you? Are you
willing to lay it all down, or just certain convenient parts of it...are
you going to put to death all claim to what this life has to offer...
abandon all thought of conducting your own affairs again...crucify
every attitude and motive of your own?*

The singular importance of this moment of truth reveals why

Jesus rebuked Peter after his triumphant confession. Because the necessary next step after that realization is self-denial and death. Peter's will was not yet entirely given over to childship. He recognized who Jesus was but remained unseeing of what it meant.

"Peter, you are looking through man's eyes, not God's," says Jesus. "Things are different in God's kingdom. My Father will conquer sin by invading the enemy's house—not with an army, but with Sonship, by obedient abandonment of the will of a Son into the will of a Father. Peter...we are going to die."

The decisive question always arrives:
What are you going to do with the freedom of
choice God has given you?

"And he began to teach them," says the gospel writer. *"The Son of God must suffer...be rejected...and be killed."*

Is it a literal death to which he calls us? Not usually. For most of his followers, it is death to self, to motives of self, to attitudes of self, and to the rule of self rather than actual martyrdom.

This may in fact be more difficult. For the death is to independence...to rights...to rule. It is a death that lasts a lifetime.

The prayer of Christlikeness, therefore, always leads to the garden.

WHAT DID JESUS TAKE WITH HIM
INTO THE GARDEN?

On the night before his death, when Jesus entered Gethsemane, his disciples sat down, one by one, and went to sleep. Finally Jesus was left alone. As he walked farther into the garden's depths, there sinking to his knees in anguish of spirit, what did he take with him? He possessed something that night. What was it?

He possessed the same free will that God had given to Adam's race in Eden. And that human freedom was about to reach its climactic perfection.

We now approach holy ground, the pinnacle of what human life can and should and was intended to mean. Are we willing to boldly venture into Gethsemane with Jesus, then up the hill of Calvary, there to discover the childship in which we are called to live?

I say "boldly" because to really grasp our Lord's ultimate prayer requires that we accompany him into the garden. But when he rises to meet the arresting crowd, to us has been given another call than that lived out by those who were with him that night. We are not to fight his enemies with words and swords and deeds. Jesus means us to stay behind in the garden, to learn from what we have just witnessed, sinking ourselves to place our own knees into the imprint left behind by his in the ground.

It is in the faintly visible impressions of the Lord's knees in

Gethsemane that we are meant to live in discipleship. It is by the prayer of not-my-will relinquishment that we will conquer, rather than with words and swords and deeds.

We are to live in the reality of the garden.

THE POWER TO CHANGE A WORLD

What an incredible thing that the Founder of our faith conquered sin by emptying himself of self. What an unexpected weapon to deal the death blow to sin—self-denial!

Peter drew the sword and would fight sin by might. Judas would attempt to manipulate the divine will into an earthly mission against Rome's rule.

But not the man who was a perfect Son.

"Put away your sword, Peter," says Jesus. "Do not lay up for yourself treasures on earth, Judas. My Father's kingdom will conquer differently from what you imagine. Not with worldly might, but in the simplicity of childship, which is nothing more nor less than not-my-will relinquishment of self."

I call it an incredible thing because, after twenty centuries, Christ's followers are still seduced by the examples of Peter and Judas that night in the garden, seeking to change the world in the Lord's name by might and money, by the power of the sword and the power of the purse, attempting loudly and visibly to overpower unbelief with "the Word of God." But after all this time, it still has not occurred to us that he would have us silently overpower unbelief with Christlikeness.

There is only one way to change the world. But it is the one thing we as his people have steadfastly not done. We have not followed his example into childship, into relinquishment of the will.

It is easy to proclaim the gospel. It is difficult to die to self.

It is easy to draw the sword. It is difficult to lay down the sword.

It is easy to preach. It is difficult to be silent.

It is easy to exert the will. It is difficult to relinquish the will.

It is easy to stand tall in the face of opposition. It is difficult to bend the knees and live in garden-relinquishment.

Put away the sword, Peter, and all who would follow in his footsteps. The world will not be changed by might but by childship.

A HARD-WON SONSHIP

The marvel of the thing continually overwhelms me when I manage to get my brain around it, that God placed free will in the center of creation.

Not only did he give us free will as a gift, but when that gift went wrong in the first garden, he allowed free will once again in the second garden to be the means of our deliverance.

It strikes me as an enormous risk on God's part. The first Adam was also God's son. God gave him self-will, knowing that it *could* be fatal. And indeed that first Adam chose self-will and independence rather than obedience, thus bringing sin into the world. The experiment with Adam *was* fatal.

With the failure of Eden so catastrophic, therefore, why did God not send an angel, or even his Son in the visible form of Godness, to redeem the world and make certain nothing would go wrong again?

A man had failed once. Why wouldn't God have said, "I will take no chances this time with the weak human vessel that was so unreliable when facing Satan in Eden."

But God entered the human form *himself* and worked the reconciliation of the universe through that amazing thing he had given only to the human creature in all the universe—*free will.*

He would accomplish salvation through Sonship. A Sonship won by the self-willed, freely chosen abandonment of independent rule.

All creation hung in the balance when Satan came to Jesus in the desert, and later when Jesus entered the depths of the garden to face the foe again. Jesus could have succumbed. The urge to give up was a real temptation.

His was no automatic Sonship. Jesus had to win the Sonship battle exactly where we do—in the will of his personhood.

He went all the way to Calvary fighting that internal battle, knowing that he didn't have to die, that at any time he could call down twelve legions of angels to deliver him.

But he fought that battle for us so that we, too, could become sons and daughters of sacrificial childship, so that like him we would have the courage and strength to pray in our own private and unseen Gethsemanes, "Not my will, but yours be done."

THE ULTIMATE EXPRESSION
OF HUMAN FREEDOM:

The will is the most individual aspect of personhood we possess. To give it *back* to the Creator, yielding it again into his hands, represents the *perfect* expression of human freedom. In such a self-willed abandonment of the right to self-rule do we reach the crowning apex of human personhood, the culmination of what we each were meant to be.

Having achieved adulthood, mature manhood and woman-hood, to now *give up* our right to them, to lay them down for the *greater* privilege of becoming children again, can be seen by the world only as the ultimate idiocy.

But in the economy of God's kingdom, it is the path to ulti-mate freedom.

We cannot be sons and daughters of Christlikeness any other

way. This is where childship is born, in our wills. In laying these wills on the altar, we rise to the blossom of our being. It is an altar not made of stone, but which is placed tenderly before us by the outspread, loving hands of the Father who gave us the ability to choose in the first place.

When we give our will into God's hands, he gives personhood back to us, infused and filled with *his* life in place of the meager selves we abandoned to him.

> *To yield the will to the Creator represents the perfect expression of human freedom.*

It is this yielding of will that Jesus came to model to us. In him does such relinquished life come to flower. In him are we made alive to the same potentiality. It is this new life, created by the Lord's obedience, that we are called to share as God's children.

Only to man has been given this glorious opportunity. Though exampled by Jesus, we must enter into this relinquishment-life ourselves. He has birthed the possibility, but only as we sink to our knees in our own invisible Gethsemanes, whispering the sacred words with him, do we bring his life alive within ourselves.

When we rise, not merely having said "Not my will, but

yours be done," but going out into the world to exist in the moment-by-moment truth of not-my-will relinquishment— *doing* that Father-will—then indeed have we joined ourselves in oneness with God to become true sons and daughters of our true Father.

A FUTURE TURNED OVER TO GOD

I have never faced death. The garden moments of my life have been quiet and inward—invisible prayer-battles against my own will. No one has followed me into my private gardens nor heard my whispered *not-my-wills*.

Such it is with we who follow our Lord Jesus Christ. His story has been told that the whole world might know of that triumphant garden prayer and be strengthened to follow its towering example. But most of your not-my-will moments, and mine, will represent a succession of tiny steps toward spiritual maturity seen by none but the Father's eyes.

The prayer of relinquishment takes many forms. Emptying our hearts of self-motive may not always occur in crucibles of anguish. I have faced such moments when tears have accompanied my prayers. But the most memorable, because it was the first, came for me on a day of quiet contentment. Perhaps the

Lord knew I was not yet ready for the Gethsemanes I would later encounter. In his tenderness, he allowed my first experience of relinquishment—like a human blossom he was carefully nurturing to make it strong enough to withstand later frosts—to be a gently progressive one.

I was a young man at the time, twenty-two and just graduated from college. My life was at a youthful crossroads. I could see little of what lay ahead. Not a single element of what would ultimately comprise my future was yet visible. The idea of writing books had no more occurred to me than going to Mars. I had not yet met the young lady who would become my wife. In short, I had no idea what was to become of me. And the uncertainty was gnawing at me.

A number of options sat on the horizon: two jobs I had applied for, the possibility of more schooling, the idea of missions or the ministry. Several important relationships that were at critical points were weighing on me, as well as the inevitable financial pressure of wondering how I was going to survive.

In the midst of this uncertainty, I went off with two friends on a long-planned trip to Europe for the summer. There we mostly worked on the small farm of friends I had made two years before.

The three months of the summer represented my crossroads. College was behind me. When I returned—or even *if* I returned, for one of the options I was considering was to remain for further schooling in Germany—I had no idea what direction my life would take.

So I was doing a lot of praying about what I should do...and about what God wanted me to do. One day as I drove my little VW bug south through Norway on our way back to Germany after two weeks in the north, one friend beside me and another in the backseat, a quiet calm seemed to settle over us.

In my own case, I found myself reviewing my life and reflecting on all these crossroads situations—jobs, money, schooling, marriage, relationships, ministry, even whether to return home at the end of the summer.

I didn't know what was best to do, or even what I wanted to do. One by one, after thinking them through, I found myself placing each specific situation before the Lord and saying, "Here, Lord—I don't know what to do with this. I put it into your hands. Do your will in this area of my life."

All relinquishment prayers are different. Mine of that day were prompted by no impending cross. I spilled no tears nor drops of blood in saying, *Not my will, but yours be done.* It was actually a very peaceful day, full of quiet joy. Without realizing the full import of it, I was turning over my right to determine the course of my own life. For is that not what the prayer of relinquishment is, laying down the right to determinative rule?

Never have I had quite the same sense of the Holy Spirit praying "through" me, prompting me to pray in ways I didn't even know I needed to pray. I mean to imply no heightened spirituality in the event. It was very down-to-earth, as God's most important things usually are. My friends and I carried on our occasional conversations, laughing and talking together. They knew nothing of what was tumbling through my mind and heart. But I could sense that I was slowly being emptied of self.

Without realizing the full import of it, I was turning over my right to determine the course of my own life.

It was a unique experience in all my life. As the afternoon came to an end, I felt a lightness coming over me. I had turned each of these concerns, situations, opportunities, and people over to God. And I literally knew that he had them now, that I wasn't holding on to them or carrying them anymore. I wanted God to have control.

It felt good…liberating.

I had willingly and enthusiastically prayed, *Not my will. Do your will in my life, Lord.* No resistance. No heels dug in to avoid the pain of the cross. I had gone to the altar *wanting* to rid myself of these burdens.

But there was one small catch.

Underlying my prayers, I assumed that the Lord would answer my prayers by giving me what I wanted. In other words, as I was praying *Not my will,* I wanted God to make sure I got the job…make the troubled relationships work out happily…and perfectly set up various other circumstances of my future to my complete satisfaction.

I don't know about you, but I do that all the time—often, I think, not even aware of it. I pray, "Lord, I turn this situation over to you," but what I really want is for him to resolve the situation with the least discomfort to me.

When we find ourselves stuck in a financial pickle, I pray, "Lord, I turn this crisis over to you." But what I am really saying is, "Give us money!"

Now maybe praying for money in certain circumstances is exactly the right thing to do. I have done so many times. But let's be honest with God and with ourselves and pray, "Lord, we need money—please provide." In order to truly turn a situation over to him and place it entirely in his hands, we are saying, "Do your will, even if it means *not* providing the money."

In other words, the prayer of *not my will* is a very, very different prayer from *Lord, please provide*. Both are valid and important prayers in the life of the disciple…but very different prayers.

So as I prayed that day in earnest, youthful zeal, was I really giving up each of these situations and circumstances and relationships, truly emptying myself and *relinquishing* them into God's hands? Or was I secretly saying, "Lord, I haven't been able to get these things to work out, so I turn them over to you to work out…*but make sure you work them out with results that are satisfactory to me.*"

But the Lord took me at my word, and I am so glad he did.

GOD'S BOWLING BALL

When we reached Germany and arrived back at the farm the next day, a stack of mail was waiting for me. Half the letters, it seemed, written a week, two weeks, and in some cases three weeks earlier, contained specific and definite resolutions to situations I had given to the Lord just twenty-four hours before. The answers had been on the way long before I had even prayed the prayers!

But in every case the answer was no!

Two letters represented a worsening of shattered relationships. The pain in my heart as I read them cut to my depths like a knife. Another was notification of a job opportunity that had fallen through. Another, I think, had to do with my school plans.

I don't even remember all the specifics, only that the devastation I felt was total.

I had given my future to the Lord, and he had taken it... taken it away!

The most apt image that comes to my mind to describe that moment is to picture all the elements of my life set up like bowling pins. Unknowingly the day before, I had handed the ball to the Lord. And he had thrown a perfect strike! I could feel and hear the shattering of the pins as they crashed in every direction about me.

As I stumbled alone out of the farmhouse and walked toward the fields, the slate of my life was suddenly clean. Devastatingly clean, as from a furnace blast. The future about which I had been praying the day before...vanished without a trace. Gone. All I felt was emptiness.

Yet as I sat down on the stone edge of a small bridge over a stream some distance from the farmhouse, something new slowly began to steal over me. That was simply the presence of God and a keen sense of his love for me. A new peace began to fill me, deeper and more pervasive than what I had felt the previous day. I was truly in God's hands now! Completely!

Had I really prayed for something I didn't want?

No. For even then, what I wanted more than anything was to be the Lord's man. If that meant having the pins all toppled so that he could take me in directions I could not yet see, then of course I wanted it, pain and all. Perhaps my prayer of the previous day had been filled with youthful naiveté. Perhaps I had not foreseen the consequences. Yet my words, *I give these things to you,* truthfully represented the desire of my heart. I think that is why God prompted me to pray them and why he answered them as he did. My saying, "Not my will—do *your* will in my life, Lord," gave him the opportunity to set my future along the path of his design. How lovingly, if painfully for a time, he dealt with me. And how grateful I am for that experience.

Do I consider it a bitter thing that the pins of my circumstances were sent crashing about by God's bowling ball? Not for an instant. God's will is a good will. I would not go back and reset a single one of them if I could. God's way is always the best way.

Almost within weeks, I discovered new vistas opening up— within my heart at first, in wonderful new ways toward God himself. And then in time, as he always does, he began slowly guiding me toward that future about which I had been so concerned.

But henceforth the journey was along different paths than I could possibly have envisioned...because it was *his* future now.

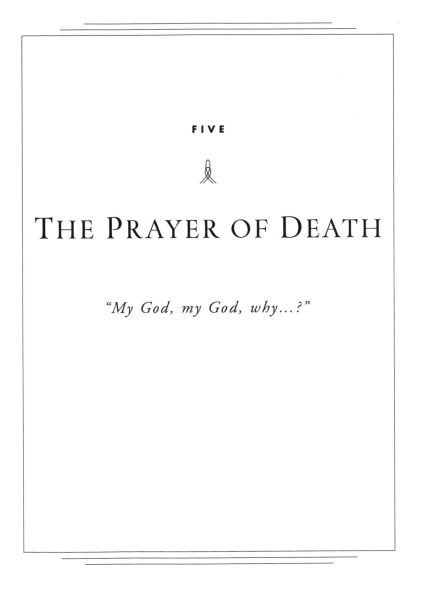

FIVE

THE PRAYER OF DEATH

"My God, my God, why...?"

When Jesus left the garden, his course was set. He left his *self* on the stony ground that was his altar of relinquishment. Now all that remained was for him to obey. In the obedience that followed was his Sonship perfected and was won the salvation of the world.

One final test of his manhood awaited him.

To endure the agony of the cross, you say?

But no. It may be that the cross, as pure physical torture, was not our Lord's greatest agony. Men possess in the flesh a mighty capacity to endure suffering. Men before Jesus had endured the cross. In his name, many would later be burned at the stake and worse. Even had he not been the Son of God, Jesus could have endured the cross as a mere man.

I mean to make no less of that suffering. It was a terrible, inconceivable physical agony, invented by the Romans as the most cruel form of death the twisted mind of depraved man could conjure up. Our imaginations cannot even fathom what it must have been like. Nor can we think that this torment was any less for Jesus because he was the Son of God. His divinity in no way reduced the pain.

Yet that physical torment may not have been our Lord's greatest test.

THE DEEPEST AGONY

Indeed, the suffering of Jesus Christ mounted to its most awful when his *will* that had triumphed in the garden began to sink into the despair of darkness and felt itself…alone.

In every moment of his life until then, Jesus had been aware of his Father's presence. In the desert facing Satan, the presence of the Father was with him. In the garden, strengthening him even as his will was crushed by the weight of what was coming, that Presence was with him. Until the cross, there remained one element of the human condition that Jesus had not yet experienced—he had not felt what it was *not to know if God was there.* He had never been filled with that universal human perplexity of looking up and feeling the heavens *empty* above him.

Thus, as he told his disciples the night before, that it was better for them if he go away, perhaps the Father, too, had to withdraw his presence during his Son's desolate hours on the cross, so that Jesus might drink the cup of his humanity to the full. And to the senses of the perfect Son, who had never been without the Father, the horror of aloneness must truly have been terrible.

His friends flee. The enemy whispers again into the ear of his tormented brain. And now even the Father's very presence steps away, grows silent, and leaves him to himself.

What will Jesus do?

Will he at last, as man is always tempted to do in his darkest hour, curse God and die? Or will he, our example to the end, exert his will even in abject darkness and aloneness, and arise and go to the Father?

Thank God! We know the answer.

He turns to God!

THE FINAL TRIUMPH

Even in the Lord's cry, "My God, my God, why have you forsaken me?" which some read as a final giving in, I read a majestic climactic shout against Satan's lie.

In the midst of Christ's desolation, when we must imagine that even his hope was gone, when his former place at the Father's side must have seemed a haunting mirage that had never been, when he wondered if he had been deceiving himself all his life, thinking that everything he had done and said and lived for was in vain...even then he cried out to God!

His God was still his God. Even in forsaking him, he was no less his God. Jesus would still turn to him and cry out to him.

Away from me, Satan! Even though he forsake me, yet will I trust my Father!

Thus, even in what looks to him as abandonment, the Lord summons his will to cry out in the purest form of faith—faith that exerts itself when no feeling or reason remains to bolster and sustain it. He has triumphed over life, over Satan, over his own humanity. Now, on the cross, he triumphs even over aloneness.

He will not curse God and die. He will instead call out to God and die—die by placing himself, always and to the end, in the hands of the Father whom he trusts.

A reader once wrote a condemning letter about one of my novels because a certain principal character, a minister, had struggled with various elements of doctrinal belief. Readers, she wrote, need authors who share their faith, not their doubts.

Though he forsake me, yet will I trust him!

I found myself wondering what she does when her Bible reading brings her to the books of Job and Ecclesiastes, or what she makes of the heart cries of the psalmist in the midst of his despair. Or what she thinks when she reads this cry from the mouth of our Lord on the cross:

"My God, my God, why…?"

It is because honest men and women of God, and even Jesus himself, cry out to the Father in their questions and doubts that their prayers get so deep into us and help us through our own seasons of darkness.

The last two utterances from our Lord's mouth, according to Mark and Luke, to my mind cannot be read but as one—as a majestic final cry of trusting death.

"My God, my God, why have you forsaken me? Yet into your hands and none other I commit my spirit."

EXERTING OUR OWN WILLS IN FAITH

It is easy indeed to look to God, rejoice in him, and give testimony to his goodness when the sun is shining and fresh fragrant winds are blowing through the mind, invigorating thought and action. When feelings and spiritual sensations run high, it is easy to look up, sense God in the heavens, and say with a smile and a heart full of praise, "My God." Even in certain kinds of trial and pain, or when failure bucks up the nerves and senses to new dedication to God's principles, it may be relatively easy to look to God and trust him to bring a new dawn. For when hope remains, one can pray for strength to endure.

But when the heavens empty of Presence; when no answering whispers return the word of prayer; when all feeling, all strength, all hope vanish in the blackness; when depression, discouragement, despondency, and despair swallow up the heart and soul and mind...what then?

When belief is gone, faith is gone, hope is gone, and love is gone...what then?

When God himself seems gone...what then?

What then is this? It is time for *faith* to exert itself. Faith that cannot *see*...yet still *wills* to believe and arises and goes to the Father and cries, *"My God!"*

It is a common misunderstanding that spirituality at its highest is experienced when God is moving within, stirring and goading and leading and guiding us to heights of spiritual fervor and activity. This error is running rampant in today's Western church. In truth, we witness a great practical lesson in this last great trial of our Lord's life, making it an integral component of the prayer of Christlikeness: *God may also appear to remove his hand from us.*

Not to test us. Not to put us through trials of suffering to make us strong, although it does have that effect. Not because he doesn't want us happy. And not because he will not make good come of all things.

He does so to give us the opportunity to exert our wills in that purest form of faith as the Lord did on the cross—to go to God *without* inner urgings and promptings and emotions, to go to him though the heavens *seem* empty and quiet above us, to go to him completely from within our *own* wills.

Not because we are led to do so…but simply because he is our Father.

Not for the blessings he will bestow on us…but simply because he is our Father.

Not living as Christians because of this experience or that experience…but simply because God is our Father.

Not rejoicing in the wonders of the Christian life and answers to prayer…but, in darkness and aloneness, turning to God simply because he is our Father.

Late in his life Hudson Taylor, the great missionary to China, commented that as the years went by he seemed to feel God's presence less—and that more was required of him in pure faith and obedience.

This is the highest form of faith—faith that *feels* not, *sees* not, *hopes* not, *knows* not, *experiences* not. When all forsake us, perhaps for a season even God himself, faith still requires us to arise with Jesus and go to our Father.

When feeling forsakes us, when answers to prayer forsake us, when God's voice forsakes us, when stirrings to worship forsake us, when hunger for God's Word forsakes us, when blessings forsake us, when the desire after Christlikeness forsakes us, when prayer forsakes us, when gratefulness to God forsakes us, even when our own will seems to forsake us and we are consumed by the low, mean, paltry *self* of our old man…even then to cry out, "My God!" and go to him simply because he is our Father.

Of course, he never forsakes us anymore than he forsook Jesus that day. Perhaps it is a poor choice of word, but I use it here because it is the word Jesus used in the prayer of death. "Seems to forsake" is perhaps the phrase we should employ.

> *When all forsake us, faith still requires us to arise with Jesus and go to our Father.*

This is what seems to me the bankruptcy of modern-day teachings based on God's blessings. What will believers so taught do when the spigot of "blessing" ceases to flow, when spiritual experiences no longer carry us along on their crest, and the evidences of God's presence run dry?

They will find themselves unfit for the times that lie ahead, sluggards grown fat on the rich food of blessing rather than warriors grown sinewy and strong for the battles that are surely coming to the people of God. Faith based on *blessing from* God rather than *trust in* God is, in reality, no faith at all. For remember, "faith is the assurance of things hoped for, the conviction of things *not* seen" (Hebrews 11:1, NASB).

The vital question, therefore, is, Has *faith* been instilled by worship and blessings and experiences and healings and praise and memories of spiritual highs? It may in fact be that true Christ-like faith is missing altogether in a life seemingly overflowing with visible blessings from God. Be very careful what and whom you revere in the Lord. Do not necessarily honor those whose lives appear anointed with visible "blessing," but rather honor those spiritual veterans with true *faith*—the capacity to trust God in the darkness.

The spigot of blessing will always, at some point, run dry. It is simply false teaching to say otherwise. God does bless those who obey him, but not always with such blessing as many erroneously teach. His ultimate desire is that we *know* him. It is a scanty "knowing" that comes by blessing alone. Thus, in the end, he always leads those who would truly know him to the cross, that they might exert their wills, with Jesus, in the purity of faith.

WHEN ALL IS GONE... "MY GOD!"

George MacDonald explains further:

> So long as we have nothing to say to God, nothing to do
> with him, save in the sunshine of the mind when we feel
> him near us, we are poor creatures, willed upon, not

willing; reeds, flowering reeds, it may be, and pleasant to behold, but only reeds blown about of the wind; not bad, but poor creatures....

The truth is this: He wants to make us in his own image, *choosing* the good, *refusing* the evil. How should he effect this if he were *always* moving us from within, as he does at divine intervals, towards the beauty of holiness? God gives us room to *be*; does not oppress us with his will; stands away from us, that we may act from ourselves, that we may exercise the pure will for good.... He made our wills, and is striving to make them free; for only in the perfection of our individuality and the freedom of our wills can we be altogether his children. This is full of mystery, but can we not see enough in it to make us very glad and very peaceful?...

Thus the will of Jesus, in the very moment when his faith seems about to yield, is finally triumphant. It has no feeling now to support it.... It stands naked in his soul.... The sacrifice ascends in the cry, My God.... It was a cry in desolation, but it came out of Faith.... The divine horror of that moment is unfathomable by human soul. It was blackness of darkness. And yet he would believe. Yet he would hold fast. God was his God yet...

See, then, what lies within our reach every time that we

are thus lapt in the folds of night. The highest condition of the human will is in sight, is attainable...when, not seeing God...it yet holds him fast.... Then first, thus free, in thus asserting its freedom, is the individual will one with the Will of God; the child is finally restored to the father; the childhood and the fatherhood meet in one...and the prayer of our Lord is answered, I in them and thou in me, that they may be made perfect in one. Let us then arise in God-born strength every time that we feel the darkness closing, or become aware that it has closed around us, and say, I am of the Light and not of the Darkness...his heart is glad when thou dost arise and say, I will go to my Father.

Will thou his will. Say to him: My God, I am very dull and low and hard; but thou art wise and high and tender, and thou art my God. I am thy child. Forsake me not. Then fold the arms of thy faith, and wait in quietness until light goes up in thy darkness. Fold the arms of thy Faith I say, but not of thy Action: bethink thee of something that thou oughtest to do, and go and do it, if it be but the sweeping of a room, or the preparing of a meal, or a visit to a friend. Heed not thy feelings: Do thy work.[2]

---

2. George MacDonald, "The Eloi," *Unspoken Sermons, First Series* (Eureka, Calif.: Sunrise Books, 1988), 172-8.

One Soul's Dark Night

My first time through this book, and the second and even the third, this chapter ended with the preceding quotation. But when my wife read the manuscript, she said, "This chapter is harder to follow. It's not personal. There is no *you* here. It's not as clear. You need to share from your own heart how you have applied this prayer."

There was a very simple reason why I had written about the prayer of death as I had. I did not want to share my own moment of deepest darkness. I didn't want to remember. I didn't want to relive that day again. For I did not "apply" the prayer at all. I only felt it coming out of the depths within me, unbidden and unsought.

Even now, as I sit in the quiet stillness of early morning, contemplating my wife's words and asking the Lord, "What would you have me do...shall I write of it?" I do not want to cast my gaze back upon that time.

The blackness fell upon me during a single day five years ago. The legion of details leading to it are irrelevant for our purposes. Suffice it to say that on that day I lost a father and I lost a son.

I lost my father, a believing man and a good man, to a quiet death. Though the final folding of the arms of his life was peaceful, it yet brought a sundering that cut deep. How could it be otherwise? He was my father and I was his son.

What I was not prepared for was the news just twelve hours later of the loss of one of my sons—not to death, but to a bitter estrangement, the relationship suddenly severed in an unexpected instant by a subtle lie he was not strong enough to withstand.

Totally blindsided, my world collapsed and crumbled at my feet. Even as I stood in the church less than an hour after hearing the devastating news, struggling to maintain my composure long enough to say a few words about my father prior to cremation, the darkness of spiritual night closed around me.

I do not know what other men experience. Did my departed father ever feel this way about me? If so, he never communicated it. Speaking for myself, I have not felt such depth of love for anyone or anything in my life as what I have for my sons. I do not say I love them more than I do my wife or the Lord, because I'm sure that is not the case. I don't even think in such terms. All loves are different, and they do not compete with one another. I only say that the physical sensation, the divine "ache" of love for my sons, has been a stronger force inside me than other loves I have felt. My love for my sons is palpable, intense, powerful.

All of a sudden I felt a huge part of me being ripped out, as if an unseen hand had plunged itself into my intestines, grabbed hold, and yanked something out of the depths of my innards. With my father's body lying in front of me, my head spun in confusion and turmoil. The pain was physical as well as emotional.

Hope was suddenly gone.

God was…gone!

Silent. Nowhere.

Something within me wanted to curse him and die. Jesus felt forsaken by God. I fear my doubt and mistrust went deeper: I felt betrayed by him.

Somehow the hours passed. My wife and I clung to each other not for comfort, but for sheer survival.

For days, all I could pray was, "God…how…why…?"

There were no more words. At first, the dark devastation was so consuming that I shed no tears. Even when they came, they were as the parched rains of the Sahara rather than the gushing flow of the rain forest. And thus even the hot tears brought no relief.

I am sorry, my friends, I have no triumphant conclusion to report to this episode, no Easter morning, no visitation of angels, no heavenly choirs, no resurrection miracle. Gradually the blackness of that night of the soul gave way to a gray dawn of stoic perseverance.

But hope for this one whom we love with all our hearts became but a distant memory. He remains immersed in a so-called

"Christian" deception—we have not seen him since, and still our hearts throb with the anguish of love.

But as I force my eyes from the black afternoon of Christ's crucifixion to what came after, I behold a truth. However difficult it may be for me to apply in my situation, it remains a truth to change a universe and give it *life:* As we die with Christ, we are raised with him to a new kind of life. His Sonship makes this possible.

But we each must nail our own hands of *self* to the cross.

"It is finished," the Lord cried. "Into your hands I commit my spirit."

The final act of trust. In the darkness of his despair, he yet trusted God to bring life. Out of that trust, resurrection life was born.

Something happened when Jesus was in the grave, something miraculous. A divine transaction occurred for which no "good life" is a substitute. There is no salvation in goodness without the cross. The cross imbues goodness with the resurrection miracle.

By the Lord's Sonship-death, we are given miraculous resurrection power, subject to the limitations of our flesh, to enter into Christlikeness with him. The first step is to pray, asking the Father to accomplish that miracle within us.

The example of Jesus is one that we can make our own. We are not called to be good worldly people, we are called to be *Christlike* people, spiritual beings, citizens of a different kingdom. We are commanded to walk with Christlike goodness, at one with our Father in the midst of a secular and sinful world.

With my eyes on the citizenship of that kingdom-sonship, therefore, I continue to pray for God to reawaken resurrection hope within me.

And I continue to pray, "My God, my God, why…?"

God is God…and he is good.

Is this an evil report, a bad confession? Will you, like the reader who wrote concerning my novel, feel that I am doing a dis-service by thus sharing my doubts and struggles rather than my faith? If so, I cannot help it.

But this I will say: Yet…I *believe*. I believe in God and in the goodness of God…and in the ultimate triumph of that Goodness.

In that belief, I go on. I can hardly call it *faith*. If it is faith, God knows.

And I go on. Because God is God…and he is good.

For I know that a resurrection followed the Lord's forsaking. And a resurrection shall follow this night my wife and I have endured. Resurrections *always* follow. Resurrection and new life is

God's way. The grave is but a figment of Satan's imagination, and all blacknesses will one day be swallowed by the Light. Whether our own light of reconciliation will come in this life or in the life to come, only God knows. We pray. But times and seasons and higher purposes are in the hands of the King.

We are not given to know what course our lives will take. We are called to be trusting sons and daughters.

Six

THE PRAYER OF LIFE

"That they may be one as we are one."

With the cry, "It is finished," the Lord's earthly sojourn was complete. Mankind's life with him, however, was only beginning.

Saviorhood had been accomplished. Lordship was now ready to change the world.

RESURRECTION CHANGES EVERYTHING

The resurrection of Jesus Christ changed the life of the disciple for all time. Until then, discipleship had been subject to physical limitations—to those who were actually with Jesus in the flesh, who saw and heard and spoke with him and witnessed miracles from his hand.

But now the possibility of that life immediately transferred to *all* mankind, no longer limited by time and space.

At first, of course, the Twelve were despondent. Not grasping what would grow out of the mighty reality of the Resurrection, they could not imagine life without Jesus beside them.

But the progression of the prayer of Christlikeness must

continue for the disciple—continue beyond relinquishment, be-yond the cross, beyond death, and into fulfilled childness, into the perfected Christ-life that Jesus' death enables us to experience.

What is this life?

Just that very life he had lived—oneness with his Father. And now that he had returned to the spirit-home of his Father's pres-ence, the life of the disciple would henceforth include oneness with Jesus as well.

"I and the Father are one," he taught.

This is the Christ-life of the disciple—oneness with Jesus and his Father.

And now such life is possible!

How true were his words when he told his disciples that it was for their benefit that he go away. Only so could he come to them in a new form, as a living spirit, no longer confined to the physical world, to be with them and in them forevermore.

He had just explained to them what this life would be like—the life of spirit-oneness. They had not understood, of course, because they were still bound by the limited responses of physical and temporal senses. But he had gone to great lengths to explain it so that they would remember afterward and then understand.

After explaining the nature of this life, in one of the most astonishing and magnificent prayers of all time Jesus prayed that his followers would be enabled to live this remarkable life with his spirit dwelling within them. And as he prayed, he gave a clear picture of what that life meant.

Step back with me then from the moving and emotional imagery of Gethsemane and Calvary, and let us return to the Upper Room an hour or two before Jesus and his disciples went out to pray in the garden. His prayer of John 17, culminating as it does the mountaintop teaching of the gospel represented by John 13–17, gives a wonderful picture of the child-life of Christlikeness.

THE BOND OF THE UNIVERSE

In considering our Lord's prayer on the night before his death, I am reminded of George MacDonald's words:

> The bond of the universe, the chain that holds it together,
> the one active unity, the harmony of things…is the devo-
> tion of the Son to the Father. It is the life of the universe.…
> The prayer of the Lord for unity between men and the
> Father and himself.… The more I regard it, the more I am
> lost in the wonder and glory of the thing.[3]

---

3. George MacDonald, "The Creation in Christ," *Unspoken Sermons, Third Series* (Eureka, Calif.: Sunrise Books, 1996), 19.

I, too, have always found myself lost in the wonder and glory of the thing. Can you imagine—with death staring him in the face, *Jesus prayed for you and me!*

If it is possible for you in this moment—wherever you are and whatever is going on around you—still yourself and quiet those many voices clamoring for your attention that would distract you from the import of these words. Let us, as it were, take off our shoes, for this is indeed holy ground, and listen with grateful hearts as the Lord's voice prays for you and me.

Holy Father, protect them by the power of your name...
so that they may be one as we are one....

My prayer is not that you take them out of the world
but that you protect them from the evil one. They are not
of the world, even as I am not of it....

My prayer is not for them alone. I pray also for those
who will believe in me through their message, that all of
them may be one, Father, just as you are in me and I am in
you. May they also be in us so that the world may believe
that you have sent me.... May they be brought to complete
unity to let the world know that you sent me and have
loved them even as you have loved me. (John 17:11,15-
16,20-21,23)

What can we do, Lord Jesus, as we contemplate your loving sacrifice, and this prayer that preceded it, other than offer you the sacrifice of our praise? Thank you that you know us, love us, and prayed for us!

What is this unity, this oneness between Father and Son that Jesus prays for us to enter into, to participate in fully with them?

It is the life he had explained only a short while before. He called it a life of "abiding" in him. And, having explained it, he now breaks out in prayer that we will be enabled to live in that life permanently.

Come with me, therefore, back yet a little further to those familiar words in which our Lord described the life of complete oneness for which he now prays.

"ABIDE IN ME"

Abide in me... These three words have always flowed over my soul like a cool mountain stream, soothing and calming and filling me with peace. Perhaps that is why, in this case, I prefer some of the older translations to describe such unity with Christ rather than the more recently rendered "remain." It is not difficult for me to imagine Jesus and his friends on that momentous night. As the disciples listen, I can envision them caught up in the wonder and peacefulness of his description of life with him. I hear his voice growing soft as he looks around at each one with eyes of deep love and then begins to speak:

> I am the true vine, and my Father is the vinedresser. Every branch of mine that bears no fruit, he takes away, and every branch that does bear fruit he prunes, that it may bear more fruit.... Abide in me, and I in you. As the branch cannot bear fruit by itself, unless it abides in the vine, neither can you, unless you abide in me. I am the vine, you are the branches. He who abides in me, and I in him, he it is that bears much fruit, for apart from me you can do nothing.... If you abide in me, and my words abide in you, ask whatever you will, and it shall be done for you. By this my Father is glorified, that you bear much fruit, and so prove to be my disciples. As the Father has loved me, so have I loved you; abide in my love. (John 15:1-2,4-5,7-9, RSV)

Ever since my early days of walking with the Lord, these few words have been among my favorite passages of Scripture. They seemed to represent the apex, the ultimate in the Christian experience, the most powerful biblical exposition of what that Christ-likeness for which I so hungered must be like. So as I prayed, *God, make me like Jesus,* it was always to John 15 that my thoughts immediately turned.

But I did not know how this "abiding" was to come about, or when I might expect to see it begin to happen in my life. It seemed somehow like an ethereal process that perhaps stole over one gradually, by spiritual osmosis. I suppose, if I were honest, I would have to confess that as dearly as I loved the passage, I did not find a great deal of practicality in John 15. The command to abide, and the description of the abiding life, filled me with peace but left me with few ideas of how it was to be done. As often throughout John's gospel, Jesus seemed to be speaking more cryptically than pragmatically.

I'm sure my shortsightedness is already obvious to you. I had not paid sufficient attention to the remainder of the passage, where Jesus explains precisely what comprises this life and exactly how one may enter into it.

Why was Jesus *one* with his Father? What enabled this oneness to be, in MacDonald's words, "the bond of the universe, the chain that holds it together, the one active unity, the harmony of things"? Jesus tells us clearly:

If you keep my commandments, you will abide in my love,
just as I have kept my Father's commandments and abide
in his love. These things have I spoken to you, that my joy
may be in you, and that your joy may be full.

This is my commandment, that you love one another as

I have loved you.... This I command you, to love one
another. (John 15:10-12,17, RSV)

Jesus was one with his Father because he did his Father's will.
To abide is to obey. And to obey is to love.

John 15 offers us a doorway, therefore—and neither a cryptic
nor an ethereal one, but one that is extremely succinct and practical—into the Christlikeness we seek. The extraordinary climax of
this Upper-Room dialog between Jesus and his disciples is the
astounding fact that Jesus prayed that *we* would enter into this life
along with the eleven who were with him at the time!

He prayed for *you*...for *me*...that we would be drawn by obedience into oneness with himself, with his Father, and with one
another.

Is it conceivable that a prayer of his will go unanswered? I
repeat, because it is so significant: *Could a prayer that Jesus prayed
go unanswered?*

OUR HIGH CALLING

Those who set themselves to abide in Christ are given a calling
higher than that of the angels. We must choose our obedience in
the midst of fallen natures and wills that want their own way.

Difficult?

Yes, indeed, it is. But it is our great privilege, our opportunity, our destiny.

This was the truth I missed years ago when dreamily reflecting on "abiding in Christ" as an emotional ideal that would somehow be infused into me by God's Spirit, causing me to begin walking an inch or two off the ground in constant harmony with God, filled with an unbroken spirit of prayer, loving everyone who crossed my path, *self* dead and buried, a radiance of purity and love shining from my face.

Jesus prayed for you and for me, that we would be drawn by obedience into oneness with himself, with his Father, and with one another.

I'm afraid something very like that is what I hoped would happen as I prayed, "God, make me more like Jesus."

Welcome to the real world, Michael Phillips!

No…it isn't a halo-life, no glowing countenance as if I dwelt forever on the Mount of Transfiguration with Jesus and Moses and Elijah. It is a practical life, not an angelic one. I must *choose* to abide in Christ, exactly as Jesus says, by loving my brothers and sisters, by keeping his commandments, by doing his Father's will as he revealed it. And continually choose it despite a self that, unfortunately, is not dead and buried at all.

If you keep my commandments, you will abide...

I am no more an angel than Jesus was. Neither are you. We are men and women. But unlike Jesus, we are weak, we are fallen, we are selfish, we are cowardly, we are timid, we are full of self-will. Yet in the midst of that humanity, we have been given the highest privilege of creation—to graft ourselves onto the vine of his life by laying down that self-will and entering into a life of abiding in his will.

The cross is a moment-by-moment way of life.

When Jesus prayed that we would be one with him, with the Father, and with one another, he was praying that we would be enabled—through our own willingness to take his garden-example as our own—to fall on our knees in the solitude of childship and say, "What, Father, would you have me do? You are my Father, I am your obedient child. Speak, and I will obey. My only will is to do your will," even when to all feeling and appearance he is not there, still to proclaim in the midst of dark desolation, *My God, you are still my God!* and then go forth and do his commands.

DAILY, PRACTICAL DENIAL OF SELF

How, then, do we abide in such childship? Of what is abiding in Christ comprised?

Of nothing more nor less than being one with the Father as he was one with the Father—by doing his will.

Jesus came to teach and example to us the specifics of that will. We know how to abide because Jesus showed us how. He is our model. We don't need to wait for it to "happen" to us, we can go out today, right now, in the next five minutes, and abide in him—by loving one another, by turning the other cheek, by forgiving those who wrong us, by praying and fasting in secret, by relinquishing our will to the Father's, by doing good, by being humble, by putting others ahead of ourselves, by being kind, by trusting God, by doing as we would be done by, by giving more than we are asked for, by being morally pure...by walking in childness.

John 15 makes the cross a moment-by-moment way of life, not an end to life.

And yet as much as I think I desire the abiding life when I am in the isolation and sanctity of my prayer closet, the moment I go out into the world to try to live in that childlike reality, I am assaulted by resistance from the very self that I thought I had slain.

Ten thousand times a year—how many times a day!—my self rears its head trying to make me ignore the practicality of the commands that open the way into Christlikeness, hissing sly justifications against the totality of self-denial required.

Life with Christ is *death* to self.

If we think of it as something else, as a life of prosperity, enlarged borders, and worldly ease and success, we are only deluding ourselves.

A dozen murmurs an hour from the voice of self jump to the forefront of intellect and emotions, whispering that I have a right to put my own priorities first, that it is only natural for me to think of myself once in a while. The voice of self is so cunning and subtle that often I do not even recognize it, occasionally even convincing myself it is the Lord speaking.

"Quiet!" I must silently shout when I come to my senses. "Begone, away…you rule no longer. Jesus Christ and his Father determine my affairs. They set my priorities and motives and attitudes. No longer will I consult you about what I am to do or think. *Self,* I recognize you for what you are—a petty monarch concerned with the loss of your throne. But it is a throne you will not occupy again, for I have removed you from it. The seat of my will is no longer yours. I have nothing more to do with you! I reject you. I deny you altogether."

ABIDING IN CHRIST

I cannot say what it might mean in your life, but for me, to abide in Christ begins thus:

To still the flood of subtle, wrong attitudes that assault me and try to make me think according to the world's values— attitudes rooted in pride, independence, selfishness, and personal gain rather than in childness and Christlikeness...

To quell the lie of independence that is in the very air of the world, telling me I can do it on my own, I *should* do it on my own, I have a *right* to do it on my own...

To ask God to do his best for those who have hurt and wronged and spoken against me, to forgive them myself, and to go down on my knees and beg forgiveness for those occasions and relationships where the wrong lies with me...

To welcome rather than resist the submission of childness...

To lay down the ambition to rise in the world or in the eyes of others, to lay down cherished hopes and dreams of achievement, possession, and success...

To trust the Father for those I love, and to trust him that all will come right in the end...

To use the weapons of warfare God has provided me to combat melancholy, impatience, rudeness, judgment, discouragement, whining, despondency, complaint…

To meet those I encounter this day with the fruits of kindness, goodness, acceptance, graciousness, humility, generosity, peacefulness, gentleness, cheerfulness, and the simple friendliness of Christian love…

To calm worry, fretting, haste, frustration, covetousness, disappointment, envy, heartbreak, irritation, and other such persistent attitudes of mistrust that hound me from morning till night…

To open my eyes to the wonderful qualities in those around me; to see others as God sees them; to recognize what they are becoming in God rather than merely what they are at this moment, remembering what I once was myself, giving them the same grace God has extended to me, rejoicing in the good and looking beyond the rest; and to love them as he loves them…

To behave toward others as I would have them behave toward me…

To actively try—though crowds and noise and profanity and selfishness and immodesty and wealth all clamor about me—to remember that I am a citizen of a different kingdom…

And to welcome, rather than run away from, opportunities to whisper, *"Not my will, Father…but yours be done."*

I cannot do these things on my own. As I have confessed before, I am a weak and frail vessel. I have not faced sacrifice, scourging and death, torture, utter aloneness. I have faced nothing in my life so difficult other than the ache of a father's heart—difficult enough, God help me, but why should I not feel it? God's heart aches for his children too. Why should I desire less for myself? Certainly I have faced nothing to compare with what Jesus endured on my behalf. The ease of life in this modern, western culture in which I find myself is appalling. The blessings God has bestowed on me are enormous, far more than I have any reason to expect.

I am given strength in the knowledge that Jesus prayed for me…and is praying for me still.

And yet…still I complain and rail and resist, as if the level of self-denial required by the abiding life were more than I could bear.

But it is only difficult to lay down wills that want their own way.

Therefore, when I sink to my knees and the practicality of Christlikeness is set before me, the first prayer I always must sigh is, "Lord…I fail so entirely to do these things of which I speak. Please help me!"

And then I must arise and go forth and live in the Christlikeness that has been commanded of me:

If you love me, you will keep my commands. If you obey my commands, you will abide in my love, just as I have obeyed my Father's commands and abide in his love. This is my command: Love one another.

As I do, I am given strength in the knowledge that Jesus prayed for me. And as his life is eternal, I have every reason to believe that he is praying for me still, and that his prayers must all be answered:

My prayer is not for them alone. I pray also for those who will believe in me through their message, that all of them may be one, Father, just as you are in me and I am in you. I pray for Michael Phillips. May he also be in us, and be one with you and with me, so that the world may believe that you sent me. May all believers everywhere be brought to complete unity to let the world know that you sent me and have loved them even as you have loved me.

Seven

THE PRAYER OF JOY

"That they might have my joy

fulfilled in them."

I took a brief respite after the last two chapters and found myself contemplating what should come next.

"How should this book arrive at a conclusion, Lord?" I asked. "How ought these prayer components of Christlikeness be summed up and put into a perspective that will make them practical realities in our lives for years to come?"

Almost immediately the words filled my mind: *the prayer of joy.*

OBJECTION

To say that this phrase was from somewhere beyond my conscious mind would be a huge understatement. Nothing could have been further from my imagination. How could *joy* culminate a discussion in which we have focused our thoughts toward Gethsemane, Calvary, and self-denial? I could not imagine how these particular words, "the prayer of joy," could have come to me. I hadn't been thinking within miles of joy. I couldn't remember immediately whether joy was even part of any prayer Jesus had ever prayed.

Quickly I began to protest.

The first objection that sprang to mind was my own lack of qualification to address the topic. How could I write about joy? My life has never been one of radiant sparkle and effervescence. I'm not one of those bubbly, bouncy Christian joy bunnies—outgoing, exuberant, cheerful to excess, and always "up." I am intellectual rather than emotional. Quiet, timid, reserved.

The Lord should know that, I said to myself. He gave me my personality and temperament. He is well aware that the most persistent battles in my walk are against depression and discouragement. I do my best to remain optimistic and walk with head high, but it is often a struggle.

These facts perhaps explain to some degree why the prayer of Christlikeness resonates so deeply with me. Indeed, at this particular juncture in my life, Gethsemane is far more real than joy.

My conclusion was straightforward: I simply didn't know enough about joy from personal experience to possibly address it adequately.

"If there is one thing I cannot write about now, Lord," I said, "it is joy. Please let me end this book in some other way than that."

My objections began to remind me of Moses and Jeremiah. Yet in my case I hoped maybe the Lord would cut me a little more slack than he had them.

But just in case, I typed the words on top of a fresh page: *The Prayer of Joy.*

Then I reread John 17. By this time I was not surprised by what I saw.

There it was—*joy!*

How could I have read right over it and not even noticed?

"Holy Father," Jesus prayed, "protect them by the power of your name...so that they may be one as we are one.... I say these things while I am still in the world, *so that they might have my joy fulfilled in them....* My prayer is not for them alone, I pray also for those who will believe in me through their message."

The Lord had my serious attention now!

I added the words, *that they might have my joy fulfilled in them,* to the chapter title, printed the page, laid it aside, and waited. He had my attention, but still I wondered if this might be one of those cases in which the Lord only wanted to see if I was willing to obey but would not really make me carry through with it.

I continued to look at that sheet while I worked on other portions of the book. Over the next few days the sense grew stronger and stronger that the prayer of joy—in a way I did not yet apprehend—contained a divine energy source to enliven and energize the other components of the prayer of Christlikeness. It was not until even later that I remembered the words Judy had had engraved on the inside of my wedding ring: *That your joy may be full.*

"Lord, what do you have to say?" I asked. "What is the joy you prayed for? I do not understand it. I do not know if I even feel it. What do you have to teach me? I am willing...but you will have to show me what it is you want to say."

And gradually, over the next few days, I began to sense the answer to my prayer.

WHAT KIND OF "JOY" DID JESUS FEEL IN THE UPPER ROOM?

One of the first things I noticed when I reread John 17 is that Jesus spoke with the Father about his joy being fulfilled in us, just as he prayed that we would be one.

Suddenly it hit me as if I had never read it before—*Jesus prayed for me to walk not merely in unity but also in his joy!*

My particular temperament doesn't matter. Whether I am intellectual or emotional, social or timid, outgoing or introverted, experiencing happiness or sorrow—none of that matters.

The simple fact is, *Jesus wants his joy to be fulfilled in me.*

This was a staggering thought—perhaps a truth I had not paid enough attention to. I was well familiar with the Lord's prayer of John 17. How many times had I read this wonderful passage? But, always, it was oneness and unity that jumped out at me—never joy.

So I began to ask myself: What could be this joy Jesus speaks of?

Was it merely the definition we usually think of—gaiety, elation, bliss, a feeling of pleasure and satisfaction...a collection of pleasant sensations that puts smiles on our faces?

Jesus prayed for us to walk not merely in unity but also in his joy!

I'm sure most of us have heard, "We're not always happy as Christians, but we always have joy." That's a good enough idea as far as it goes, pointing out a component of joy deeper than mere happiness alone. But let's face it, the two are almost interchangeable. When we say joy, we're still talking about an emotion, a feeling of exhilaration and gladness and delight. Maybe it's a deeper kind of feeling, but it is happiness nonetheless. We're still talking about having smiles on our faces.

Is that what Jesus meant?

To try to discover an answer, I found myself wondering what Jesus himself was feeling at the moment he spoke of his joy: *That they might have my joy fulfilled in them.* What did he mean? What was going on in his own heart right then? Wasn't he about to be betrayed? Wasn't he headed to the cross? What joy?

Picture the situation clearly. The Last Supper had concluded. The Upper-Room dialog with the Eleven was nearly done. In a few minutes they would leave the house and walk down into the Kidron Valley and up the other side to the Garden of Gethsemane. We really don't know, but in all likelihood it was between ten o'clock and midnight.

This was when Jesus said, "I say these things…that they might have my joy fulfilled in them."

Within an hour or two, Jesus' agony of mind and spirit would be so great that he would sweat blood and beg his Father for release from the dreaded cup that was approaching.

Did he feel what we commonly call "joy" in the garden? How could he have? The Bible says he was in "agony of spirit," not happiness. Agony of spirit is hardly joy.

Within another hour or two he would be arrested.

Twelve hours after that he would be hanging on a cross.

A few hours later he would be dead.

Was Jesus ecstatic and happy to watch his disciples flee? Was he smiling with pleasure as the nails were driven through his wrists? Was he exhilarated and rejoicing to feel abandoned by God?

Of course not. One cannot read the scriptural account without concluding just the opposite—that his sorrow and mental anguish, not to mention sheer physical torment, were positively excruciating.

Yet, with all this staring him in the face, he speaks of his joy being fulfilled in us.

The only conclusion I could draw is that he must have meant something very different from what goes by the name of "joy" in my mind. I don't think he was feeling a great deal of happiness in those moments.

I continued to search the Scriptures for insight. The mystery deepened even more as I placed Jesus' words alongside other statements about him and the life that comes to his followers:

[He was] a man of sorrows and acquainted with grief. (Isaiah 53:3, NASB)

He has borne our griefs and carried our sorrows. (Isaiah 53:4, RSV)

He was wounded for our transgressions, he was bruised for our iniquities. With his stripes we are healed. (Isaiah 53:5, RSV)

My soul is overwhelmed with sorrow to the point of death. (Mark 14:34)

And being in anguish…his sweat was like drops of blood. (Luke 22:44)

You will be…persecuted and put to death, and you will be hated…because of me. (Matthew 24:9)

Grief does not equal joy.

Sorrow does not equal joy.

Wounds do not equal joy.

Stripes from a lash do not equal joy.

Anguish does not equal joy.

Persecution does not equal joy.

How do we unify all these with Jesus' desire that his joy be fulfilled in us? It seems a little like the old saying: "If that's how a friend treats you, who needs enemies?" I can imagine someone looking at the above list and thinking, *Phew, if that's what the joy of Jesus is like, I'd hate to be around when the trials start!*

EMOTION OR STATE OF BEING?

I consulted a few of my Greek texts. No immediate light bulbs went off. The word Jesus used in John 17 was simply "joy"— χαρα, *CHARA*.

As I dug further, however, a fascinating truth began to reveal itself.

I saw that the intent of the Greek language contains both an emotional and an intellectual component.

Pause and think about this for a moment. If you are accustomed to thinking of joy as I always have, then the second half of the equation—the intellectual side—may be a new twist for you. However I may have distinguished joy and happiness until then, there was no doubt that my perception of joy was always as a felt emotion of the heart

Most of us have given lip service to the fact that joy is supposed to transcend feelings. But practically speaking, we expect the Christian life to generate regular smiles of exuberance or we start to think something is wrong. In other words, however differently joy might manifest itself, we still consider it an emotion—as something to be *felt*.

Suddenly, here was light shining in from a new angle—from the *brain* and not just the *heart*—joy not necessarily always as something to be felt, but as a state of mind.

Some evangelicals are afraid of the word *intellectual*. But it is important to distinguish the distinct roles in faith occupied by the mind and the heart. In this case, I found it extremely liberating to recognize that joy perhaps has a much greater and more stable intellectual component—existing in and flowing out of our intellect rather than solely out of our feelings—than I had recognized.

Am I "glad" to be alive? Of course. Do I always *feel* that gladness? No. But even then, I am still glad to be alive. I still live in a state of being glad.

It is the difference between my home itself and the things inside my home that makes my life more enjoyable and pleasurable. Those things can change or be given away, sold, replaced, or stolen. I enjoy those things—my most comfortable chair, the tea mug that perfectly fits my fingers, my favorite pen, and our bed at night—even though many of them change through the years. We are sleeping on a different bed than we were using two years ago. The pen with which I am going over this manuscript right now is less than a year old. And I am notorious for breaking mugs!

The things inside the house that I enjoy, and that bring me joy, change. But we have been living in the same house for almost twenty-seven years. It is our home and it remains our home despite the changes that may take place inside it.

That's what I mean by living "in the state" of being glad. That is my home. I am glad to be alive. I live there.

But the *feeling* of gladness, and the specific things that may make me feel gladness throughout the day—are just the changeable things inside the house.

When the sun is shining and blessings are apparent and trials are not pressing about me and all of life seems pleasant, the smile on my face corresponds to the joy of gladness in my heart.

But there are other times when life is hard, when the sun is not shining, when discouragement overwhelms me, and I cannot see God's presence through the fog. My feelings are downcast, but I am still glad to be alive, glad to be God's child, and glad that my life has meaning in the midst of such emotional valleys.

Thus, gladness as a component of joy is both emotional *and* intellectual. I *feel* glad (emotional), and I *am* glad (intellectual). It represents something that comes over me emotionally from time to time, as well as a state of being in which I exist permanently.

Some people may say that they are not glad to be alive. But I am.

Gladness for life is always my home, whether the sun is shining or not.

THE HOUSE OF JOY

Recognizing these distinct components of joy—one that originates in the *brain* and another that originates in the *heart*—unlocked a huge door in my understanding.

In perhaps the same way that we say "I feel glad" and "I am glad," perhaps we can also distinguish between "I *feel joy*" and "I am *in joy*"—I live *in the state of joy* regardless of my feelings at any given moment.

Then another question occurred to me—and whether this strikes you as momentous or not, it was huge to me: Is there also a "house of joy" in which I could dwell *all the time*—a permanent state of being that describes who I am and where I live in God— even though my roof might occasionally leak or I might lose a favorite pen or break a favorite mug?

Gladness for life is always my home, whether the sun is shining or not.

Was it this *house of joy* that Jesus was talking about, rather than the things of joy that come and go and change inside the house?

Was it this house, this state of being where Jesus dwelt with his Father, that he prayed for us to dwell in as well?

Obviously, when Jesus said, "I am very sorrowful," he was not feeling gladness or joy. But his *state of being* remained thankful to be the Son of God. He was not glad *of emotion,* but he was glad *to be.*

He still dwelt in the house called *Joy* with his Father.

Perhaps here we begin to apprehend a little more closely what

Jesus was thinking at the time he spoke with his Father about his joy being fulfilled in us. He was about to enter the garden "exceedingly sorrowful." He was on his way to die.

But his state of being was at peace. His spiritual dwelling place was intact because he knew who he was. He was at peace with who he was and with what he had been called to do. And he trusted his Father to remain with him.

PEACE, SERENITY, CONTENTMENT, THANKFULNESS

Investigating yet further, I discovered a linkage between the Greek word *CHARA* and peace, serenity, and contentment—a *state of being* that is at rest in the Fatherhood, sovereignty, and love of God.

Now I began to get a sense of what the walls of this house were made of—this dwelling place, this state of being called joy.

By being at rest in God, we're not talking about spiritual lethargy but about the peace of God—being in harmony with oneself, with God, and with one's place in God's purpose and plan, unflustered by circumstances, by change, by trials, by ups and downs, or by fluctuating feelings.

Peace, serenity, contentment, thankfulness, tranquility, trust, composure—such make up the walls and floors and roof and supporting timbers of the dwelling place called joy.

And here I believe we at last begin to unlock what it was that Jesus prayed we would dwell in—a state of being that is at peace with our childship in God.

Clearly it was in such a state of joy that Jesus lived. And the walls of this house remained strong—though sorrow, anguish, and even crucifixion would pound against it.

AT-JOY-NESS

What did Jesus feel the night before his death?

I believe he felt "at-joy-ness." He felt peace in the state of being one with his Father, peace with who he was as the Father's Son, and peace with what he had to do.

Jesus desires for us to abide in a house of at-joy-ness, serenity, and trust, a home of eternal joy.

He was sorrowful. The emotion of joy was not proceeding out of his heart. He *felt* no joy. But he *dwelt* in joy. *At-joy-ness* was still his home. He was at joy…at peace…content, serene, thankful to be the Son of his Father.

THE PERSPECTIVE OF ETERNITY

As I prayerfully reflected on that night before his death, my thoughts now turned to what Jesus was feeling, not about himself in anticipation of his own sufferings to come, but toward his disciples...and toward us.

One cannot read John 13–17 without sensing a great tenderness and love in Christ's heart toward these men who had shared life with him.

The full dimension of his prayer, it seems to me, is revealed in his earlier words to them: "Do not let your hearts be troubled. Trust in God; trust also in me.... Peace I leave with you; my peace I give you" (John 14:1,27).

This is the house in which he desires for us to abide—a house of at-joy-ness, serenity, and trust, a home of eternal joy that enables his Sonship to rest in his Father. His prayer was that we would dwell in the state where the same peace that characterized his Sonship would also characterize ours.

It is a place where the perspective of eternity reigns, the capacity to look beyond this earth, beyond everything that is of this world, knowing it to be temporary and passing.

Was not the Lord's own peace that night founded in eternity being ever-present within him? He was not overpowered by what he was about to suffer. Eternity lay just on the other side of the cross. His peace transcended whatever this world could throw at him—the lash, the crown of thorns, the nails, and the cross.

His trust was in God, his Father, a good Father who is sovereign over all.

The perspective of eternity.

I say these things while I am still in the world, I now hear Jesus praying for me, *that they might live continually in the state of being that sustained me in Sonship, serene in your will, Father, at joy in your care, content in your love, and at peace…because they trust you as I trust you.*

ANOTHER PRAYER

I stepped outside to walk and breathe deeply and try to let these new thoughts sink in. I was not consciously praying. But my brain and heart were quiet. As I went, I felt something almost like an invisible weight slowly lifting from my shoulders. Not a heavy or oppressive weight. It was very subtle. Actually it didn't weigh much at all, but I could tell that something was happening.

For thirty-five years I had been praying the prayer of Christlikeness. Yet there had remained within me the subtle suspicion that a tiny corner of my spiritual being was still just a bit out of sync and didn't feel "the joy of the Lord" as it should. What

Christian doesn't occasionally suffer from the illusion that we're supposed to be up and happy and cheerful every moment?

Now that misconception slowly vanished in the wonderful new reality of the prayer of joy, in the realization that joy was a house in which I might dwell—at peace in my sonship. I no longer had to worry about whether I *felt* joy—I could simply dwell in that state of *at-joy-ness* even if the roof did leak from time to time. I was free to enjoy the things of the house, knowing that they did not contain the source of joy anymore than the pen or keyboard I might be using is the source of this book.

I am at peace, I said to myself as I walked, *even in the midst of certain heartbreaks that remain painful and real. I live in the house of joy in the same way that I am glad to be alive. Thank you, Lord, for this revelation.*

Perhaps it was not a new peace I sensed, but a recognition of something that had existed all along. I would be no one other than who I am. I would be nowhere else than where I was at that moment. I was God's child, God's son, and in that fact I was at rest.

As I returned to my office, I thought that perhaps the prayer of Christlikeness for me was indeed being quietly answered.

And I was glad.

Lord Jesus, I prayed, *help me to know not only your sacrifice but also your joy. Thank you for this glimpse into the state with your*

Father in which you dwelt and had your being. Teach me to rejoice, as you commanded me, in the serenity and peace of at-joy-ness.

Deepen within me not only the life of relinquishment, but teach me also to carry myself with the joy you knew, not walking with head bowed as I grimly follow my own Calvary road, but with head high because I am God's child. Teach me to not merely obey but to obey with rejoicing, looking beyond, living in eternal expectation that good-ness reigns throughout the universe.

Help me to abide in you, and in oneness with you, in such a way that allows your joy to be fulfilled within me. Let me take my own obedient share in that abiding life by rejoicing as the Father's obedi-ent child.

Father of Jesus, let me allow you to carry out your complete pur-pose within me and through me, that Christlikeness itself might be fulfilled in me. Let the prayer, "What would you have me do?" be ever on my lips and in my heart. Let my will be only and always your will for me. Let the words, "Not my will, but yours be done" be the constant orientation of my heart. Make me one with you as you and Jesus are one. As you make Christlikeness more a part of my being and character, let obedience be my only desire. And when darkness closes around me, let me still cry out in trust of you, My God.

Deepen more and more aspects of your joy within me—let it be, as Jesus prayed, fulfilled in me—that I might thereby bring more completely to reality in my life the prayers of Christlikeness, childship, relinquishment, death, life…and joy.

And throughout what remains of my life, Father, through the years and in the small moments of this very day, fulfill your purpose in me, and continue your work…to make me like Jesus.

To share your thoughts with the author,
to receive a complete listing of his books, or to inquire about
LEBEN
a periodical featuring writings, reviews, articles,
reader letters, and devotional thoughts from Michael Phillips,
as well as writings and essays concerning the work of
George MacDonald and his legacy, please contact:
Michael Phillips
LEBENSHAUS INSTITUTE
P.O. Box 7003
Eureka, CA 95502